CHOSEN VESSELS

WOMEN OF COLOR
KEYS TO CHANGE

Rebecca Florence Osaigbovo

 Dabar Publishing Company

Unless otherwise noted, all Scripture quotations are from the King James Version of the Bible.

Scripture quotations marked (NIV) are taken from the Holy Bible, New International Version ®. Copyright © 1973, 1978, 1984 by International Bible Society. Used by permission of Zondervan Publishing House. All rights reserved.

Quotations on pp. 45, 46 and 140 from the book, *Blessing or Curse: You Can Choose* by Derek Prince, copyright © 1990 by Derek Prince. Used by permission of Baker Book House.

Quotations from *The Spirit of God's Kingdom Newsletter* copyright © 1991 by River of Life Ministries, P.O.Box 10102, Cedar Rapids, Iowa, 52410. Used by permission of Francis Frangipane. All rights reserved.

Lyrics from the song, *It's Our Time* copyright © 1989 by Dr. Myles Munroe. Printed by permission of author, Dr. Myles Munroe: Faith-Life Music, Nassau, Bahamas. All rights reserved.

Publisher's Cataloging in Publication
Osaigbovo, Rebecca.
   CHOSEN VESSELS: Women of color, keys to change/ Rebecca
   Osaigbovo.—1st ed.
      p. cm.
   Includes bibliographical references
  ISBN 1-880560-60-7 (cloth).---ISBN 1-880560-57-7 (pbk.)
    1. African American Women-Religious Life-Christian Theology I.Title
  E185.86 1992 / 301.242 / Church library:258.843
  Library of Congress Catalog Card Number 92-85567

PRINTED IN THE UNITED STATES OF AMERICA

To my niece, Vanessa Florence, who is alive today because of the prayers of others. Also to her sister, brother, cousins, and all in her generation whom God is seeking to bring forth as a praise to His holy name as our generation learns to make the Lord our God.

To God be the glory!

Acknowledgments

I thank God for the team He put together to produce this book. My sincere appreciation to the following members who agreed to read the manuscript at various stages and gave helpful feedback: Gregory Alexander, Charles and Lynne Brown, Betty Dresser, Pete Dresser, Wanda Dykes, Malettor Cross, Deborah Edwards, Clarinda Gibson, Cynthia George, Shelia Hoerauf, Linda Moore, Sam Oleka, Lynne Sajna, Andrell Sturdivant, and Brenda Watkins.

I am indebted to Diane Reeder of Written Images, a key player who was able to guide the manuscript to a polished product with her professional content editing skills. I appreciate Maureen LeLacheur, Evelyn Marshall, and Joyce Stephens for their capable assistance in editing and proofreading.

I am grateful for the artistic skills of Lynette Gibson (cover design and inside illustrations) and Faye Gipson (cover illustration). Without the typing and transcribing skills of Bridget Jordan and Denise Jones, I could not have gone very far.

Thanks to Andrew LePeau of InterVarsity Press and Horatio Bennett of MetroPUBLISH for coaching and technical assistance.

Finally, every team needs a fan club. The biggest star on the team has been more than the captain of the fan club, but a coach, friend, assistant, advisor, and more. I especially thank God for my loving husband, Uwaifo Osaigbovo and the rest of the family fan club—Esosa, Esohe (Rachel), and Nosa.

To the others who cheered us on—the many friends and relatives who prayed, encouraged, and believed, thank you.

Foreword

Rebecca has broken the long silence of African American women. Over the years we have heard millions of voices babbling about the state of the Black woman. People (primarily men) offer their theological opinion on the subject; radical feminists have even thrown in their two cents worth. Everyone in our society is telling the Black woman what she should do. The question arises, who should she listen to?

In CHOSEN VESSELS: *Women of color, keys to change* we finally hear a voice from the inside; the voice of an African American woman speaking to other African American women. In this book, Rebecca provides a road other women can follow in helping to restore the Black family to a Biblical foundation. In our current society, the Black woman must find healing in order to be empowered to regain a positive role in her family. In this way, both she and her family can profoundly and positively affect American society.

Unfortunately, some of our young Black males—perhaps out of frustration—have turned against Black females and are brutalizing them verbally, emotionally, and physically. This book gives examples of a Biblical standard that can be adhered to in the midst of this abuse and degradation.

Rebecca speaks out in defense of a Biblical view of the American Black woman. CHOSEN VESSELS will help to change the way Black women see themselves, and the way they are viewed by society. It will also help affirm our dignity as a people. This book is timely, and so needed at this time when more and more of our families are broken, and many headed by females.

CHOSEN VESSELS is not just a book for African American women. It goes further than that—it deals with the great issues that are so prevalent in the day in which we are living—ones which our society as a whole needs to hear. This book should be exposed to all other ethnic groups as well as to every African American family.

Rebecca, I commend you for taking a strong and noble stand at this critical time in the history of our people. I commend you for setting a theological view for women of color. May God richly bless you and may this book be received greatly throughout all our nation.

John Perkins
Publisher of URBAN FAMILY Magazine

Preface

Why have our cities detriorated? What lies behind anger, frustration, violence, and self-destruction? What has gone wrong in this nation?

How could understanding the past, present, and future of African American women give us some answers to these tough questions.

No one simple answer exists to all of the problems in this nation, but a consideration of the spiritual dynamics—both positive and negative—of African American women is critical to the process of moving toward change. Understanding God's purposes for women and the sabotaging of those plans for African American women *will* point us to some answers.

Though everyone can be involved in bringing change to this nation, regardless of race, sex, or national origin; this is an invitation to African American women to participate in an unique opportunity in God's plan to also be keys to major change.

Though many share the blame for the state of our families, cities, and nation, I write this book because I believe women of color do not have to wait for others in order for things to get better. The buck can stop with us. We can give the next generation a heritage of blessing. This book shows WHY and HOW. I also write because. . .

> Blessed be the Lord my strength, which teacheth my hands to war, and my fingers to fight....That our sons may be as plants grown up in their youth; that our daughters may be as corner stones, polished after the similitude of a palace. That our oxen may be strong to labor; that there be no breaking in, nor going out; that there be no complaining in our streets.... Happy is that people, that is in such a case: yea happy is that people, whose God is the Lord. (Psalm 144:1,12,13,15)

Contents

Dedication
Acknowledgments
Foreword
Preface

Section one: The problem

Section two: Healing process

Section three: Praying for others

Section four: Putting it together

Appendices

Section one: The problem

Chapter 1

Beginnings

In the beginning God created the heavens and the earth. **Genesis 1:1**
The Lord God formed man of dust from the ground and breathed into his nostrils the breath of life; and man became a living soul. **Genesis 2:7**
Now the serpent was more crafty than any beast of the field which the Lord God had made. And he said to the woman, Indeed, has God said, 'You shall not eat from any tree of the garden '. . . When the woman saw that the tree was good for food, and that it was a delight to the eyes . . . she took from its fruit and ate; and she gave also to her husband with her, and he ate. **Genesis 3:1-6**

To get a good handle on spiritual issues, let's go to the very beginning. We'll start with God. He is *the* positive spiritual reality. God was before time and is beyond time. He created time, the earth, and all that is in the earth. God is above all and it is by Him that all things exist. He currently holds up everything by His Word (Hebrews 1:3).

Next we'll look at God's created beings. At a specific point in time, God created beings that are called angels.

One angel holding a high position in God's kingdom decided he wanted to take God's place. He persuaded one-third of the angels to side with him as he led a mutiny in heaven. This was the first conflict. But it was impossible for a created being to be over the Creator, the One who always was. As a result, God had to kick him out of His kingdom (Luke 10:18). In fact, he was sentenced as a punishment for his insubordination; but his sentence was not immediately carried out.

As much as we would like to deal with things we can see, behind many of the problems in our cities is an army of unseen personalities. The commander-in-chief, the same one who tried to overthrow God, is a deceiver. He is called Satan, Lucifer, and the Devil. He wanted God's place as ruler; he does not want any of God's purposes to work. He is God's opponent. In opposing God, he has become the negative spiritual reality.

This angel is still waging a losing battle against God. Though the two are in conflict, there is really no contest between them. It's like an ant trying to subdue an elephant.

If the conflict were directly between God and Satan, there would be no match. However, the conflict is indirect and quite dependent upon the responses of a third party.

At another point in time, God also created human beings to be objects of His love and to carry out His purposes. Humans, with a free will that Satan works diligently to manipulate, are the center of the conflict between God and the adversary.

The deceiver knows God loves humans. He is jealous. He hates humans because they are made in the image of God and have the potential of becoming co-rulers with the Son of God, Jesus Christ. He knows we were created with the ability and destiny to defeat him.

Consequently, all of Satan's wrath is poured out on the human race. He is as much an enemy of humans as he is an enemy of God. He knows he can hurt God most by hurting humans. He desires to keep us at odds with God and close to himself so we are recipients of curses and not the goodness of God. He desperately wants to keep us unaware of our ability to overcome evil with good. Because then he would be subdued.

Ultimately, he is behind all of the chaos in our cities and world. He is behind all oppression. His strategy is to keep everybody from knowing and operating in their God-ordained purpose and power.

Why was humanity created?

The next chapter will go into more detail about the enemy of God and humankind. But first, let's look at God's original plan for humans. People were created for several reasons. They were created to praise and worship God; fashioned to commune and fellowship with God; made to manifest the life and character of God into this earth and bring glory to God. And as already noted, they were designed to be recipients of God's vast love and affection.

God formed the first person out of the dust of the ground and breathed into that form the breath of life. The combination of God's breath with the ground created the third part of Adam, his soul (Genesis 2:7).

Actually, the Hebrew word for "living" is the same word used for God's breath. God's breath became man's spirit. Essentially Adam became a spirit/soul. The soul, comprised of the will, mind, and emotions, was the key to humanity.

The soul is so special to God. Jesus once said to the multitudes, "What does it profit a man to gain the whole world, and lose his soul?" (Mark 8:36). The soul allows us to freely love God. Within the soul is the power of choice. It also distinguishes us from programmed robots who only do what God wants.

The soul is also very important to God's enemy. The soul is the enemy's gateway to access and control.

God did not intend for humans to have a knowledge of good and evil apart from a relationship with Himself. He did not want them to live their lives based on their thoughts or feelings. The soul was to be energized and ruled by the spirit. Man's spirit was designed to contain the life of God. God's Spirit connected to man's spirit was to be a winning combination!

God planned great things for the first couple, Adam and Eve. He gave them a good world, and only desired the very best for them. Adam and Eve had dominion over the whole earth. They in turn were to carry out their responsibilities, depending on God for overall direction.

It was critical that, in connection with God, Adam and Eve use the authority and characteristics endowed upon them by God to reign over the earth and carry out all of their duties.

God planned for mankind to reign over the very enemy of God, defeating him and his plans. Man was to bring destruction to God's enemy by executing the judgements written against him (Psalm 149:9).

The first choice

God gave the first couple a free will to love and obey Himself from a position of conscious choice. He desired men and women of like mind with Him, not robots. God strictly forbade Adam and Eve from eating of the tree of the knowledge of good and evil. This was the choice test. This was the point in which they could exercise their own free will. They were told the consequences if they chose to disobey: separation from God in death.

If they ate of the tree of life, the first man and woman would have maintained their connection with an infinite God who knew all things. If they ate of the tree of the knowledge of good and evil, they would no longer have the Spirit of God overshadowing their own spirits. Separated from God, decisions would have to made based on the principle of the knowledge of good and evil. They would be forced to live by their thoughts and feelings, by what their physical eyes and ears discerned. No longer having the benefit of the God of all wisdom and discernment as their covering, they would be subject to anything in the spirit arena. Instead of being spirit/souls, they would become body/souls, ruled by their flesh.

According to Genesis, chapter 3, the enemy of God tricked mankind over to his side. This is what happened:

- Satan divided mankind by getting Eve by herself. Remember God gave Adam and Eve the dominion together to rule over the earth and all that was in the earth. Satan knew that dividing weakens the whole.

- Satan deceived Eve. He lied to Eve about what God had said. He insinuated that God was holding out on them and told her she could run her own life if she took of the tree of the knowledge of good and evil.

- Eve influenced Adam to eat. Remember this because you'll hear it again in this book: women have a tremendous power to influence.

- Humanity moved away from a dependence upon God. The soul operates from the flesh if it does not draw its strength from the spirit as empowered by God's Spirit.

God's plan: before the foundation

God already knew before time how He was going to get truth to mankind. Before the coming of time, God had a plan. Even if the one who opposed God would be the god of this world and his system the dominating force, God was confident He could convince mankind His way was better. God had a plan to give mankind another opportunity to choose the tree of life.

In the beginning, God provided His very own life to be in and upon Adam and Eve. They lost that protection when they sinned. At the point of independence from God, death occurred. Separated from the life of God, His outer covering of glory was lifted, and they became naked (Genesis 3:10).

God has given us the opportunity to regain the covering Adam and Eve lost for us through His Son, Jesus Christ. If we partake of everything available to us, we will have the ability to overcome the enemy not only in our lives, but in the lives of our families, friends, and neighbors. God provided everything necessary through the life and work of Jesus.

The second choice

Adam and Eve made their choice. They ate the fruit. Now we are paying the price. But we too have a choice. We can decide we do not like the enemy's evil ways. We can choose the tree of life through Jesus Christ.

In this period called time, the question is: who will we believe? Will we believe God is good, has our best interests at heart, and is worthy to be trusted without condition? Or is God evil, not to be trusted and unworthy for us to give over our lives to unconditionally? Will we believe the enemy has the best deal for us? Is God to be praised, and the enemy damned, or is God to be cursed and the enemy let off the hook?

Let us close this chapter by reemphasizing this important fact: God is good and only desires the very best for all His children. African American women especially need to see how the deceiver has lied about the goodness of God. We will go behind the scenes and look at how the enemy keeps us from the blessings of God in order to make God look bad.

We can choose to whom we will direct our loyalty. It is essential for us as African American women to give our lives over to God unconditionally. As long as there are questions about God's goodness, or even His ability to do the right thing, lurking in our emotions, we will never give our lives to Him in radical obedience.

Let's face it, the enemy has not gotten any stronger. God still has two thirds of the angels on His side. Why don't we get out of the enemy's hands, away from his plans, and become tools in the hands of a mighty God?

We would do well to let God take over our whole lives. We have made a mess trying to manage them on our own. Even those of us who have invited Him into our lives really need to let Him take full control.

The whole issue is one of control. The problem we have with God is we would rather keep reign over our own lives, while God requires being in complete control. Let's say we are convinced that we need a new manager for our lives. What would we want? We would look for someone who would know the job, had a lot of experience, was available, and we could afford.

Someone wants the job. God has forwarded His resume to us: the Bible. Why don't we go over a brief synopsis of His qualifications and give His offer some serious consideration?

GOD

Everywhere, All over, Every Place   (123) 456-PRAY

Anytime

Dear Friend,

I heard you were considering a new manager for your life. I would like to apply for the job. I believe I am the most qualified candidate. I am the only One that has ever done this job successfully. I was the first manager of human beings. In fact I made them, so naturally I know how humanity works, and what is best to get people back into proper working condition. It will be like having the manufacturer as your personal mechanic.

If this is your first time considering Me, I would just like to point out that My salary has already been paid by the blood of my Son, Jesus on the cross of Calvary. What I need from you is the acknowledgement that the price is sufficient to pay for all of your sin and your independence from Me. I need you to believe this in your heart and to tell somebody else about your decision with your mouth.

The next thing I ask is the right to change and fix your life so you learn how to stay close to Me. I will make some major changes and revisions. They are not for you to worry about. I need your permission to execute these changes My way and in My time. I will change your desires and give you the strength to make the changes. Please keep your hands out of the way. Don't try to help Me and don't resist Me. I really do need your full commitment and cooperation. If you give Me those, the process can go smoothly, without delays.

Yours Sincerely,

GOD

P. S. I AM. I created the heavens and the earth. I CAN.

GOD

<u>Resume</u>

Experience: From the beginning of time. Before the beginning of time. From everlasting to everlasting.

Ability: All powerful.

Prior Employment: Created the universe, put the galaxies in place, formed man. Established heaven and earth by My spoken Word and am currently holding up the world by My power.

Education and Training: I am and I have all knowledge.

Character References: Love, light, and life (1 John 4:16, 1 John 1:5, John 14:6). A representative, but by no means conclusive list of other character traits follows:

Wisdom	James 1:5
Comfort	2 Corinthians 1:3
Truth	John 8:32
Healer	1 Peter 2:24
Strength	Philippians 4:13
Forgiveness	1 John 1:9
Provider	Philippians 4:19
Mercy	Ephesians 2:4
Just	Romans 3:26
Good	Matthew 19:17
Peace	Romans 14:17

Availability: Willing and ready to take over your life. Able to put your life back together again. Will bring all of who I AM into your life. Can start now. Will transform your life if you let Me.

Salary requirement: Work in your life has already been paid for through the blood of My Son, Jesus. Your only responsibility is to commit initially and on a daily basis to trust and obey what Jesus has done and wants to do in your life.

Other references available upon request

Chapter 2

The real enemy

How you have fallen from heaven, O morning star, [Lucifer] son of the dawn! You have been cast down to the earth, you who once laid low the nations! You said in your heart, "I will ascend to heaven; I will raise my throne above the stars of God; I will sit enthroned on the mount of assembly, on the utmost heights of the sacred mountain. I will ascend above the tops of the clouds; I will make myself like the Most High." But you are brought down to the grave, to the depths of the pit. Those who see you stare at you, they ponder your fate: "Is this the man who shook the earth and made kingdoms tremble, the man who made the world a desert, who overthrew its cities and would not let his captives go home?" Isaiah 14:12-17 NIV

African American women have an enemy who does not want them to realize he is the source of many of their problems. Separate plans have been instituted against women and African Americans to make them less than God intended them to be. This enemy has sought to put all who would commit their lives to God out of commission. But he has especially sought to keep African American women away from God's purposes.

The purpose of God's Spirit in any group of people is the same: conforming individuals into the image of Jesus. However, the actual process will be unique for different cultural groupings. God has a specific message to African Americans that counters the plans of the enemy against them.

What is the thrust of that message? God wants to confront and root out deeply ingrained lies of insignificance. He wants us to see ourselves as recipients of the grace of God. We can then give of ourselves from that grace and be a force for change in the kingdom, and in the world.

It is time for African American women who may have felt left out to find out the special place reserved for them. All need to stand in the victory secured by Jesus. The real war has already been won.

God said He would pour out His Spirit upon all flesh. All the members of His family are being made ready to work together in the oneness needed for a victorious army. This chapter will provide an expose on the enemy so we can move out of his hands into the care of our good Father God.

This true enemy of African American women knows when African American women wake up to fight him, his fate is doomed. So he has put into operation a plan to make African American women ineffective. He has made them feel inferior and beyond God's use. He has tricked them into fighting the wrong war—against other "imagined" enemies. As a result, a sizable portion of the army designed to defeat the enemy is not fighting him.

We can win battles if we just realize God can use the plans of the enemy for His own purposes as He prepares His army to reap a harvest. Trained warriors are needed to go into enemy territory to release prisoners. Think of it as "boot camp." Many African American women are in this boot camp, but have not understood how God could use the special difficulties they face.

As I see the pain, anguish, and complaining of African American women going through boot camp, it has become clear to me that not understanding God's purposes only prolongs the anguish. It is my hope that insight will help women use their painful experiences to properly direct their anger at the real enemy and their energy to rescue those caught up in his prisons.

Facts about the devil

The devil is a liar and is the father of lies (John 8:44). The truth is not in him. However, he does have an advantage: because of what Adam and Eve did, we often believe the lies he has to say concerning God, and about what is good for us. Satan is also a spirit. We cannot see him but he is very real. He operates behind the scenes, but is clever at getting his job done. His main talents are trickery and deception; he is a master magician who specializes in delusion.

The deceiver has a lot of help to carry out his plans. He has a well organized army doing most of his work because he cannot be everywhere as God can. His help are the angels who joined with him in the rebellion against God. They are called evil spirits or demons. They catalog our weaknesses and plan how to arrange circumstances to make us angry at God, thus bringing us under their influence. One of their most successful ways of hurting humans is their ability to operate through others.

Fear, the opposite of trust, attracts these unholy angels. They know us so well, it is easy for them to use circumstances and people to get us to stop trusting God. They know what makes us fearful, irritated, independent, and essentially what moves us away from God and into enemy territory.

The "Germ Theory"

I watched a video about hand washing techniques for hospital workers several years ago, and an idea struck me. Satan and his helpers are like "germs." They infect people, but can be "washed away" with the right techniques.

In the physical world, germs are everywhere. But how many of us are preoccupied with them? We do not get concerned about germs until our own defense system is weak. Of course, we are more susceptible when we are in the presence of someone who is infected and is spreading their germs by coughing or sneezing. Under these conditions, we try to protect ourselves.

The same can be said for "spiritual germs." They are everywhere. Jesus is the only defense against "spiritual germs". Any person who has not received Him is infected already. A person who knows Him, but is not walking close to Him has their defense weakened.

The earth is full of people infected with "spiritual germs". These people are sick and need a doctor. The people of God have been given the commission to bring them healing. God's people have been given whole warehouses full of the "antibiotics" of truth to cure "spiritual infection". God's people have been given the mandate of demonstrating "germ free" living and introducing people to the Great Physician, Jesus Christ.

Normal, healthy spiritual people have nothing to worry about evil spirits. Those who are spiritual babies, young, spiritually sick, or who have wounds in their soul do have to worry about becoming infected with "spiritual germs." Also those who work in places that have a high density of infected people need to practice good hand washing techniques.

Passing "germs" around

God's goodness is available to those who remain close to Him; God's wrath comes to those who stay close to the enemy. Those who stay at a distance from God can also experience evil from the enemy.

Even people who have invited God into their lives are prone to wander from God's presence. We are prone to act independently and control our own lives. Independence from God is sin. Moving away from God leads to sins, the activities which either hurt ourselves or others such as lies, hatred, murders, etc.

Like fear, sin also invites spiritual germs. Sin puts a hole in the Christian's armor giving the enemy an open door to our lives and often to our descendants. Once Satan has a person under his bidding to act in opposition to God's best, that same "germ" can pass down through four generations (Exodus 20:5). This is how the sins of parents are passed on to children. All sin hurts somebody.

The enemy's plan has been to infect as many people with as many germs as possible, getting a better grip on the human race. The enemy also influences people to sin against others. That's another one of his ways of passing germs around. These evil acts build up and eventually release the judgment of God. That is what the enemy wants.

Most of us have heard about the dangers of sexual impurity, but many do not understand why this particular sin is so devastating. Sexual sin is one of the most effective ways of spreading "spiritual germs" from one person to another. It is especially warned against in the Word of God. The warnings are not meant to reduce our fun, but rather to protect us from physical disease as well as from the enemies of our souls.

How Satan gets a "foot in the door"
Someone once mistakenly left the back door of their apartment unlocked. A boy who lived in the building came in and stole some things. Most of the things were recovered, but the victim did not know the boy had also stolen a spare back door key.

The key gave the boy access to the apartment. When the residents were away from home, he came in and stole more things. Once it was discovered he had a key, the locks were changed and the stealing stopped.

Many times the enemy gets into our lives when we leave a door open by allowing unconfessed sin in our lives. When Jesus Himself is not the sole key to our hearts, the enemy can take advantage of us by using those other things to which we give our hearts to come in and out of our lives.

God has a way of letting Satan bite at our heels to keep us close to Himself. It could be compared to being in the center of a fenced field with God. As long as we stay right next to Him, we're safe from the enemy.

We will shut the door on the enemy and change the locks as we learn to remain close to God.

The enemy resides on the other side of the safety fence but is always trying to attract our attention. Often, we are deceived into thinking the other side has good things. Sometimes, we'll even get down out of God's arms to get a closer look. When we come close to the fence, Satan snaps at our heels.

Experiencing pain from the enemy is meant to send us back into the arms of God. That's the system of a good God to keep us close to Himself and safe.

The system breaks down when we experience pain, blame God, and run further away from Him. Of course the independence from God will lead to more acts of sin. Instead of admitting we were wrong and turning back to God, we often try to make it on our own.

Eventually we fall into a trap of the enemy. Soon it is a stronghold and it becomes harder to come back to God.

Indirect enticement

When the enemy cannot entice us into his territory directly, he'll try the indirect way. Imagine, for example, that someone hits you. He uses a hammer to do so. Then imagine that you take the hammer, throw it on the ground, and stomp on it.

"Stupid," you say.

The person who hit you would be happy. He may realize that you were terribly misinformed, but he wouldn't tell you.

When we focus our anger against people, it is like focusing on the hammer. Satan often uses people to carry out his plan of attack. Many even allow themselves to be used of the enemy. But for the enemy it serves as a trap to get us bitter at the person and into enemy territory.

Can Christians be infected?

That is a controversial question. The Scriptures tell us not to give place or ground to the enemy. The Scriptures tell us the enemy can aim "wiles" at us. They say that as we restore others, we should look to ourselves lest we also fall. They tell us to take our thoughts captive, casting down imaginations and strongholds (Ephesians 4:27; 6:16; Galatians 6:1 & 2 Corinthians 10:5).

Obviously, the enemy can work in our lives to make us weak and ineffective, even put us to sleep. It is also obvious Christians have a responsibility to stay clean.

It is possible for Christians to become infected with the thoughts of the enemy. These thoughts give the enemy access into our lives. When we allow thoughts that enter our minds to stay and become a way of living, we have a stronghold that needs to be "disinfected."

If we fail to disinfect properly, the enemy can come in and out of our circumstances, stealing, killing and destroying. He steals our joy, peace, and right ways of living. He brings his garbage with him, leaving it at his will.

It starts in the mind. God says we are to live in the power of His Spirit. But too often we find that our lives are motivated and energized by our mind, will, and emotions: our souls.

If you are trying to "do the right thing" without acknowledging God in all your ways and diligently seeking His face, you are living from your soul and not from God's Spirit. This inevitably leads to sin.

To say that the enemy cannot get into our lives is a lie serving the enemy's purposes. The enemy can have place, ground, and even a stronghold in our lives. We can suffer from his wiles. We can fall into his traps.

We can be infected.

Spiritual germs do not have legal right to reside in a believer's body or soul. Evil spirits have a right to attack us when we sin and to reside in unbelievers. Even though they do not have the permission to live in us, they try anyway. They do not necessarily follow the rules. And when we do not know our rights, they take advantage of our ignorance. God's people are "destroyed for a lack of knowledge" (Hosea 4:6). If we refuse to fill our lives with God's presence, some can definitely move in as non-paying tenants until evicted.

No, evil spirits do not belong in blood bought vessels of Jesus Christ. But mice and roaches will try to stay in a house as long as no one challenges them. They will also hide their presence to keep from getting exterminated.

Satan does not like us to have access to truth. He hates truth, because it destroys his schemes like boiling water melts ice. When we walk in truth, the enemy's plots are thwarted.

Though the enemy is very clever, he has no power, except what is given him. Christians have been given power over the enemy and his kingdom. Those who know Christ have the mandate of destroying the devil's works and maintaining his defeat.

Being a Christian does not guarantee victory over Satan, especially if we are ignorant of his techniques. We can give up the victory purchased for us by neglecting to forgive, participating in activities that attract evil, and by refusing to put on our armor.

The enemy is not able to trick one who stays in the presence of God. The way has been provided for us to live above all of the evil one's strategies.

How do we "disinfect"?

There are many ways of getting rid of unwanted germs. The water of the Word cleanses. Fiery trials also burn out germs, much like fever. We can change the locks on our hearts by letting Jesus singly be our heart's desire. We disinfect our minds with large doses of the antibiotic of truth. We learn to take regular spiritual baths (confession). We need to learn how to eat properly (Bible reading, study, and meditation). We all need the continuous flow of the blood of Jesus in our lives to fight infection and provide immunity to germs.

Are you severely infected? Perhaps fasting and prayer will get you started on your way to renewed spiritual health (for extended fasts of more than a day, be sure to consult with your doctor).

Satan's power and ability was stripped at the cross of Jesus Christ. That's the good news most of us need to know. The Word of God and the Holy Spirit are available to maintain the reality of what Christ did at the cross.

The Bondage Breaker by Neil Anderson is a good book to read if you want to know more about becoming free of spiritual germs.

In any case, let us get rid of the germs, the rodents or bugs in or around us. Let us get rid of the deceiver's plans against our lives. Let us be careful not to leave any "flesh hooks" for him to grab as we take back the ground we have given him.

Summary

The enemy can introduce evil into the lives of people in several ways. Let's put them all together. He can occupy ground that we have given him. He can steal the key to our hearts and use it to come in and out at will. When we sin, he can stick a "wile" in the hole created in our armor. He also can gain access to our lives by the actions of our ancestors. When he cannot get to us directly, he can work through the people around us or in our circumstances to cause bitterness, frustration, or lack of faith.

How do all of the enemy's plans relate to the African American community? Is the African American community under a curse? Is the African American community permanently blocked from the blessings of God? Is there a conspiracy against African Americans? We'll answer these questions in the next chapter.

Chapter 3

Bitter roots

See to it that no one misses the grace of God and that no bitter root grows up to cause trouble and defile many. **Hebrews 12:15** NIV

I'm tired of the black community always being put in a negative light," complained a caller to the host of a local Christian radio talk show. The host had stated that abortions were more prevalent in the African American community than in non-minority communities. The caller challenged him by referring to statistics that refuted the host's claim.

One of the questions African Americans often struggle with is whether God loves them less than others. To many it appears the blessings of God are upon other races, but His curse is upon us. Why is it that African Americans seem to suffer more? If God has loved us the same as everyone else, why has He not come through for us?

Is there a curse on the African American community? Yes, but not the kind of curse we have historically heard about. God is not the author of this curse. Its author is the enemy we spoke of in the last chapter.

As a subculture in the United States, some real differences exist between our community and other communities. We do seem to suffer disproportionately. Relatively, more of our people have AIDS. More are in prisons, hospitals, mental institutions, unemployment lines, poverty, and broken homes. These are known facts.

We should be tired of the enemy having such open inroads into our community and among our people. It is time for African Americans who know God to wake up and shut the doors of our communities to the enemy.

In this chapter we are going to consider the enemy's plan against African Americans. He has sought to make African Americans feel inferior, less in importance, less loved by God, worthless and nearly useless in the kingdom of God. Satan has used everything at his disposal, including "Christians" and out-of-context Scripture to do his dirty work.

Slavery: forming a bitter root

Most of Satan's schemes against African Americans were rooted in the experience of slavery. Much of the anger in our communities has come from a root of bitterness beginning during slavery and passing down from generation to generation.

Francis Frangipane illustrates in this excerpt from an article appearing in the *Spirit of God's Kingdom Newsletter*, June 1991:

> The enslaved soul travelled a tortuous road. All the landmarks in the individual's soul were shattered, devastated beyond our present faculties to understand, and broken beyond human abilities to repair. Having been robbed of his or her freedom, most slaves finally accepted their fate; and as they did, oppression and death soaked into their spirits.

> There were, of course, a few blacks who overcame extreme difficulties and were esteemed and respected by many whites. But they were the rare exceptions. For typically, whenever a people was taken

captive, they faced death in one of two ways: they physically died due to hardship, or they experienced death through the psychological bondage of slavery itself. You see, the spirit which manifests through the victors upon the vanquished is the spirit of death. Thus slavery exacted a quantitative and qualitative loss of life upon the blacks. It immersed their culture in a flood of death.

You know the history. In slavery, we as a people were severely wronged. Our women were raped. Our families were separated. We were used and abused. Out of the frustration and helplessness we experienced, bitterness found root in the souls of our ancestors.

This bitterness has been passed from parents to children because of no other place to vent frustration. When people are wronged by those who are over them, they will often take it out on the people that are under their control. Our disturbing tendency to discipline our children out of anger originated in slavery. This is experienced as rejection by children.

This angry discipline has continued through the centuries. Even after slavery was over, parents still had to deal with much rejection and frustration from society. In matters of discipline, they often reverted back to the example of their parents.

The inability to put together in their minds and emotions the treatment of parents, African American children often suffer from broken hearts. They know in their minds their parents love them, but have a hard time dealing with parental anger. This has in turn led to parental disrespect.

Children in African American communities grow up with a lot of pain. Comfort and affection could have healed some of the pain, but parents frustrated just trying to survive in a hostile world have little energy for affection. Add the wedge placed between men and women in our communities, and you have a situation in which it is very difficult for our little ones to have a healthy childhood.

Spiritual germs spread through the black community

Since families were broken at the will of the slave masters, the family relationship was sabotaged. It was too painful for men to really care for a woman and then be sold somewhere else. Women became objects to fulfill sexual desires. This lack of respect has been passed down through the generations.

We must also consider the problems we have respecting authority. Again, look at the pattern established in slavery. How much respect can a normal human being have for someone who treats him as an animal?

The enemy's plan has reached deep into our communities to cause pain, discord and every kind of evil. This has been his ultimate aim. His schemes are well orchestrated to continue a cycle of destruction from generation to generation.

How slavery still affects us

The *Spirit of God's Kingdom Newsletter* continues:

> Although slavery was legally abolished in the eighteen-hundreds, racism continued. Its wounds remain today in the souls of many blacks, propelling a growing percentage of young black men toward violence.

We might be tempted to say, "Well all that is in the past. We should stop dragging up old issues. Hasn't this been discussed enough? It is time we put this behind us so we can get on with our lives and be about God's business!"

But evidently, it has not been sufficiently dealt with. It took root. Otherwise, it would not still be affecting us today. The bitterness comes out today in the violence we inflict upon each other.

Again, from the *Spirit of God's Kingdom Newsletter:*

These men neither understand their actions nor can they find a way out of the shroud of death which broods over their neighborhoods.

The fact is, much of the violence in our cities today is the bitter fruit of a tree the white race cultivated in the soil of racism and slavery.

In America today one in four black males over twenty-one is in some form of incarceration. And the highest cause of death among black men under twenty-five is homicide. It is only by the grace of God, Who became the strength of the black man early in his struggle, that the remaining majority found creative and productive ways to apply their lives.

The way we harm our own bodies with alcohol, drugs, and food is one of the reasons our health suffers disproportionately. Also our bodies were not designed to house bitterness and anger. The enemy knows that. His plan is working.

We are an embittered people. Becoming a Christian does not necessarily take the anger away.

Roots of deception in American Christianity

We often wonder why it appears God's favor on this land may be running out. Why is judgement allowed in a country God has seemed to bless for so long? The way African Americans were and still are treated in this country is certainly one of the reasons. When people are hearers of the Word and not doers, they deceive themselves (James 1:22).

Once a Christian sister expressed how she did not understand why it seemed as if her African American brothers and sisters in the faith seemed to blame her for what happened in the past. She said something like, "I wasn't living back then. It wasn't my fault." At the time, I had no answer. Later, I came to realize the sins of her ancestors were still upon her.

Christianity in America is under a serious web of deception rooted in the experience of slavery in this country. It is important to see how the sins of our spiritual fathers still affect us today. It is important to look at history to understand what we have inherited. We need to know what we are dealing with. We need to know how we today can reverse the curse of what our natural and spiritual forefathers have brought.

The following quote, again from Francis Frangipane, cuts to the root of the problem. It comes from the newsletter cited earlier:

> Although we point to drug abuse and gang violence as some of the strongholds in our society, in most cases these were but symptoms of the greater problem of racism. In the genealogy of our cities' violence, cultural pride and envy begot racism. Racism begot oppression, oppression begot fear, futility and hatred. . .
>
> The Lord set a standard and put it in the spirit of America. Our founding fathers believed, and were willing to die for the truth, that "all men were created equal." They understood that every individual was "endowed by their creator with certain inalienable rights—life, liberty, and the pursuit of happiness." God has taken our own words and is using them to judge us. For we fought a war to secure freedom and then denied it to the blacks.

Racial prejudice among the people who are not of God is one thing, but the same spirit among those who claim to be of God is something entirely different. How is it that people can say they love God yet hate their African American brothers and sisters that they brought here as slaves and introduced to the God of Abraham, Isaac, and Jacob?

In *The Arrogance of Faith*, author Forrest G. Wood documents the role "Christians" had in bringing slaves to America, justifying slavery and the ill treatment of slaves and defending the "rights" of Americans to keep slavery going even when God began to raise up true ministers who began to challenge those ideas. It is tragic this is in the history of American Christianity.

Wood says racism within the Christian ranks completely compromised and "subverted" the principles upon which this country has stood, principles that emphasized peace and good will. He makes the point believers often refused to recognize the error of racism.

Eleven o'clock Sunday mornings is said to be the most segregated hour of the week. Racial barriers are so rooted in the American culture, many do not know to what extent it is present within them. Few have any idea of how much the Lord Jesus Christ hates it and is offended by it. This is one of the greatest hindrances to God's presence among His own people. Judging by outward appearances is not tolerated in God's kingdom. It is in such direct opposition to His kingdom's principles that it will have to be rooted out of Christians in America before God's presence and favor will rest upon this nation in greater measure.

Even if we feel that we have escaped or have sufficiently dealt with the problems within ourselves, it would not hurt to just ask God to search us anyway. There might be something hidden back in a remote closet that we haven't been in for years. And if we do not find anything, we still can be tools in God's hand to pray for others who still remain bound by these chains.

Much of the bias against African Americans is not conscious or overt. Unfortunately, the ingrained cultural tendencies have not been challenged enough by religious leaders. It is costly, inconvenient, and uncomfortable to make changes to accommodate those who are different. The world's system of operating advocates exploitation and continued oppression of the disadvantaged.

Racial prejudice has done a tremendous amount of damage in this county. It is a terrible offense to God. It has literally torn up His family.

Results of racism in the Body of Christ

The enemy has lies for every group. The four main lies to African American are as follows:

- God loves other races more than He loves us.
- A curse is on us strictly because of the color of our skin.
- We are inferior to others because of the color of our skin.
- Even God cannot use us.

Ingrained racial prejudice among the people of God has served to give "proof" to these lies.

As a result of our experiences rooted in slavery, unfortunately, many African Americans are put out of commission from God's army because of fear, insecurities, hatred, bitterness, unforgiveness, and resentments. The result: devastating loss in the kingdom of God.

The enemy has been very successful in causing destruction in major cities. Many Christians living in these cities are not combating the real enemy. Have you ever wondered how there can be a church on almost every corner, and our cities still are in the mess they are in? If we are supposed to be the light, why are our cities so dark?

The vicious cycle against African Americans has been in operation for decades. The barriers that remain among those who claim the name of Jesus are a disgrace to His name. Yet the cycle continues.

Partiality. Prejudice. Hatred. Bitterness. Unforgiveness. We in America will have to face up to these serious issues if we desire God to heal our nation. Though some of these things are changing, it is not enough.

Yes, African Americans may be very religious, but we have a hidden rift with God. We are angry at God. We wonder how and why

He let such injustice happen, especially since much of the evil was done in the name of God, under the cloak of "Christianity."

How is it that American Christianity could tolerate such inconsistencies for so long and still refuse to look upon racism as God looks upon it? How could the Bible be used to justify slavery and the inferiority of blacks? Why did God allow us to be slaves? Why didn't God bring us out of slavery sooner? Why is it that when blacks became brothers and sisters in the Lord they were never treated as true brothers and sisters? How is it those same attitudes are prevalent today?

No, we may not necessarily ask these questions out loud. We may not even be aware that these conflicts are in our hearts. But they are there and few have found peace to the nagging questions of WHY and HOW.

Some of the common pat answers of "American Christianity" may appease our minds for a while, but they have never satisfied our hearts. It is time we put it all under the blood of the cross. It will take change in our attitudes, words, and actions.

We may be religious as a people, but because of the pain and the hidden conflict with the God who "allowed" this, while giving lip service to Him, we often end up worshiping other gods.

We have turned to the government as our provider. We have turned to food, alcohol, sex, shopping, drugs, status, and even church for comfort. We have turned to sports, recreation, and music to get our self worth. We turn to relationships to feel secure. We have turned to all these idols instead of turning to God alone. This leads to curses and not the blessings of God.

But there is room for much hope. God often does His greatest work in, among, and through those who have been offended the most. Again, light shines best in the deepest darkness. The darkness of sin and wrong against us as a people will give opportunity for God's light to shine upon us in a bright way. Where sin abounds, grace abounds the more. In essence, our experience here can be as redemptive as Joseph's experience was for the children of Israel.

How African Americans are affected today

Yes, there is a conspiracy against African Americans. It has been cooked in hell. Perhaps there are some who actually work so closely with the enemy that they too know the whole plan. But most probably are carrying out the plan ignorantly. White American Christians have been used as pawns in the hand of the enemy to carry it out and even continue its effects until this day.

The enemy is using many to carry out his purposes of destroying our community. Along with the institutional church, the government also has played its part in the conspiracy. The government will lie to us about what is safe. To point to just one example, it will not tell our communities that the only spiritually, emotionally, and physically safe sex is abstinence until marriage. Even if it did, it does not have the power to help our young men and women maintain abstinence.

The bureaucracy of government has enough problems worrying about how to get more money. It doesn't care how many of us die. The more we die, the better. It doesn't care if we destroy our young through abortions or if we destroy ourselves through drugs. It tells us to just say "no" to drugs, not to whom we should say "yes."

Jesus took upon Himself the curse of sin. When individuals continue in sin, they are subject to the judgment of God. But right now, we will consider how people in the African American community too often judge improper judgment and curse each other with damaging words.

Christians in America justified slavery and mistreatment of African Americans. But we have not mentioned that white Americans, including those who claimed to be Christians, also cursed African Americans with their mouths. From pulpits, it was taught that blacks were less than humans. In books written by "Christians," it was proclaimed that Blacks deserved to be slaves since God had cursed them. Once again, Forrest Wood documents these facts from America's history.

Even today, you can still hear "Christians" saying all kinds of curses against African Americans. These will not be repeated here in this book. But without understanding, people say what they see with their physical eyes and ears and thus continue the operation of evil in others' lives. The words spoken against African Americans are curses. Christians today are still playing into the hands of the enemy by cursing African Americans.

Even if the words contain measures of truth, the Christian responsibility is to bless and curse not. We cannot expect those who are subject to the enemy's bidding to do anything other than his bidding. We are not talking about non-Christians. We are talking about the responsibility of those who claim to know the Lord. Christians are responsible for restoring breaches.

When we think of the fact that these curses are going against African Americans who know the Lord Jesus Christ, it is even more tragic. Members of a body would actually bite and devour other members of the same body.

Derek Prince has done an excellent job researching what the Bible says about curses. The following is a quote from his book, *Blessing or Curse: You Can Choose:*

> Both blessings and curses belong to the invisible, spiritual realm. They are vehicles of supernatural, spiritual power. Blessings produce good and beneficial results; curses produce bad and harmful results. Both are major themes of Scripture. As already pointed out, the two words are mentioned in the Bible more than 640 times. Two important features are common to both. First, their effect is seldom limited to the individual. It may extend to families, tribes, communities or whole nations. Second, once they are released, they tend to continue from generation to generation until something happens to cancel their effects . . . .

This second feature of blessings and curses has important practical implications. There may be forces at work in our lives that have their origin in previous generations. Consequently, we may be confronted with recurrent situations or patterns of behavior that cannot be explained solely in terms of what has happened in our lifetimes or personal experiences. The root cause may go back a long way in time, even thousands of years.

The main vehicle of both blessings and curses is *words* [emphasis added]. Such words may be spoken or written or merely uttered inwardly. Scripture has much to say about the power of words. The book of Proverbs, in particular, contains many warnings as to how words may be used either for good or for evil.

How can sins of American Christianity be dealt with?
Francis Frangipane who took a bold stand in his newsletter is an example of a Christian leader who is facing the issues squarely. Ministers who go public with these ideas are few and far between.

Most people want to keep the part Christians played in creating evil in African American communities under the rug. Many do not want to think about it. Few want to accept responsibility for the current plight in our cities.

Unfortunately, the author of *The Arrogance of Faith* does not take a kind view towards Christianity. Racism among Christians continues to hinder people from seeing the true God. Do we need more mockery because the only Jesus that most Americans have seen has been a false Jesus?

Christians of every color displaying love for each other will give a different testimony to the world. African American women can begin to operate in a radical, unconditional love that will bring change and healing to ourselves, our families, and to other members in the family of God. We have an opportunity to demonstrate the true Jesus. Through Christ we can reverse the curse on our families and communities. It will take the Spirit of God to bring conviction and break through the walls of deception.

For most people, the problem of racism and the effects of slavery are someone else's problem. But the sins of the forefathers of American Christianity must be confessed.

We cannot bring the dead back to have them confess their sins. But we can do as Nehemiah did: we can confess the sins of our fathers (Nehemiah 1:6). Many who were wrong were not our physical fathers, but they are still part of our family in the faith. We may be embarrassed over these skeletons in our "family closet."

It would be nice for those who have inherited the wrongs of their physical and spiritual fathers to take the lead in confessing their sins to begin the process of ridding our communities of their continuing harm. But if no one else is going to do it, we must do it. They affect us too adversely.

"You mean you're not going to talk about what the white man owes us or should do to make things right with us?" No. You'll have to go somewhere else for that. What good would that information do us? Make us feel good?

We cannot wait for others to be the solution to our problems. Nobody's problems are totally caused by the actions of others. A curse without a cause does not come (Proverbs 26:2). So when others curse us, there are ways of living above it. Our response to others' action is fundamental. God has the power to deal justly with the wrong actions of others if we follow the principles laid down in His Word.

God has ways of bringing restitution. We must be careful to let God do it in His timing. Our proper response may hasten that time. If we don't want to hear that, we can go ahead and continue to try to get others to change. But if we're serious about seeing some real changes in our communities and cities, we are going to get to some practical ways that we can change and enjoy the blessings of God even if no one else changes.

African American women and the enemy

Rejection and wounds often result in unforgiveness. African American women have been rejected much. So in many instances there is an open invitation for the enemy's plan to operate in their lives. But this does not have to continue with Christian African American women. They have the privilege of living under the protecting armor of light (Romans 13:12).

What we need to understand is that Satan is the real enemy of African American women, NOT males, whites, or God. Satan has used males and whites to hurt us, but because they have been used does not mean they are our enemies.

Someone could use a hammer to hit us on our head, but it would be ridiculous for us to be bitter and hateful toward hammers the rest of our lives—perhaps a little cautious, but not bitter. Hammers can also be put to good use.

Because Satan is invisible, we do not see him. We only see the people he has used to cause pain in our lives. But they are just hammers in his hand. We've been mad at the hammers while we have left Satan alone. African American women beat up on hammers while Satan has slipped away and not felt a single blow.

That can change. Let's focus our anger on the real enemy. Let's get our minds off the hammers. We need to recognize that everything done to us was done under the direction of the enemy. Let's turn our anger in the right direction. God can help us do it right.

We have to decide whether or not we will forgive the whites and indeed the African brothers who cooperated with the "manstealing" of the slave trade. Our response at this critical time will determine whether we will stay in prison or move to the throne room. God can break every yoke of bondage that has been put on our backs—rooted in the experience of slavery here in America.

Summary

Because we have not understood the apparent absence of God's blessing, African American Christians have a rift in our emotions that makes it difficult for us to fully trust the only One who can rescue us from the curse under which Satan has us.

Satan planned all of this. He used "Christians." The bitter roots among African Americans are a hard-to-unravel web. The solutions many bring to our community only touch the symptoms and never go deep enough. It's time to uproot the enemy out of our community.

Our community is entangled in such a mess of sin, lies, curses, bitterness, and unconfessed injustices, it will take divine intervention to deal with it all. First we should confess not only our sins, but also the sins of our natural and spiritual ancestors.

God wants to get at the roots of the problems in our community. In this chapter, we have examined the structure of these roots. Since our focus is on African American women, the next chapter will examine in detail a plan that goes back to the very beginning of time: the plan to divide men and women.

Chapter 4

Dividing men and women

And if a kingdom be divided against itself, that kingdom cannot stand. And if a house be divided against itself, that house cannot stand. **Mark 3:24,25**
And I will put enmity between you and the woman, And between your seed and her seed; He shall bruise you on the head, And you shall bruise him on the heel.
Genesis 3:15

From the beginning of time, Satan's plan has been to destroy the unity existing between men and women. After sin entered the world division became an issue. Before that the woman and man had worked together in co-reigning over the earth. They were given dominion over the earth, to subdue it. They could have both done it—together!

Togetherness: God's original plan
God made Adam singular. God made Adam the completion of mankind. The initial Adam was a unique blend of all traits and characteristics of both male and female. He was complete in himself, much as God is complete in Himself. But in being complete, he did

not have one like himself to keep him company and to love. And by himself, he could not demonstrate the importance of unselfish living.

Maybe God looked at Adam and said to Himself, "Two are better than one. . . if one prevail against him, two shall withstand him; and a threefold cord is not quickly broken" (Ecclesiastes 4:9-12). Actually, what we have recorded for us in Genesis is that God said it was not good that man be alone (Genesis 2:18). So God took a rib from Adam's side and made another physical being. God planned: "Together, they'll have dominion over all" (Genesis 1:28).

God's purpose was togetherness. He knew that united the first couple would stand. He also knew a house divided against itself would fall, and two were better than one. God was aware one could chase a thousand, but two could put ten thousand to flight (Deuteronomy 32:30). There is multiplied power when a man and a woman are in harmony, united together against the enemy.

To demonstrate the power of "two," God decided to separate Adam into two persons. God was the first to separate. In Genesis 2:21-23, we see God taking from Adam and making Eve and in the words of verse 23, "She was taken out of man."

The task at hand was to now walk in communion and togetherness in such a way they would be able to effectively rule over the earth. Both members of the couple were important. As was previously mentioned, they were to remain connected to God in all they did. God wanted their lives to be guided based on the life of God within, upon, and with them. Together, connected to God, Adam and Eve would have been able to overcome the plot of the enemy.

Somebody seeks to divide

However, someone else was watching this whole chain of events. The enemy was looking on and saying, "Yeah, but divided, they'll fall" (Matthew 5:25). He then proceeded to successfully execute a fall. Satan approached the female part of the partnership and, by persuading her to act independently of her partner, he put the first rift between the two.

The first thing accomplished by the enemy was the severing of the connection between man and woman. Secondly, he broke the connection between mankind and God.

The bond between the first man and woman was powerful. One of the most powerful keys that a woman possesses is the power to influence. This key can be used by God. This key can also be used by the enemy.

Because of the power of influence, Adam chose to follow Eve. Instead of letting her be in her separation from God all by herself, Adam joined her with full knowledge of his actions. He chose to follow the woman he loved rather than the God he also loved. Eve's influence pulled Adam out of dependence upon God and into the enemy's hand. Now Satan had them both.

When Eve and Adam ate of the tree of the knowledge of good and evil, they bit into the nature of God's enemy. So instead of being rulers over everything upon the earth, as God originally intended, they now become subjects to the rule of a new master. Satan, the enemy of God, now has the right to control and use them as tools, hammers in his hands. This was the first transfer, from God's hand into the enemy's.

God intended the man and woman to co-rule over the earth. He desired them to work together and subdue the enemy. His original plan was not totally forsaken. It was just put on the shelf until a later time.

God knew evil would be brought into the earth's atmosphere by the eating of the tree of the knowledge of good and evil. He knew that both men and women would end up tools in Satan's hands to inflict hurt and pain upon each other. Without Himself in control, God knew the enemy would seek to control things by his kingdom of darkness, and we would try to control each other.

Did God scrap His plans after Adam and Eve had deserted ship? Though the Lord had separated the first Adam into two, we see something in Genesis 2:24. It seems the Lord still wanted them to be one. The Lord ordained that they would be one flesh, and out of that oneness, reproduction would result. Obviously, God was not finished with mankind. God separated. The adversary divided. God will bring back oneness.

The threat to Satan

God's punishment for Satan's part in orchestrating the fall is found in Genesis 3:15. There we find God threatening the enemy. The Lord God says to the serpent, "I will put enmity between thee and the woman, and between thy seed and her seed."

Did you catch that? God said He would put enmity between Satan and the woman. Now we might be tempted to think, "Big deal. I'm sure the enemy is shaking in his boots." We think very little of the fact that God told His own adversary, Satan, that women would also become his (Satan's) enemy.

The emphasis has always been on the woman's seed. That is critically important. God was speaking of Jesus when He told Satan her seed would bruise his head. But also important is the point about woman herself. Though we may not see it significant that women and Satan are enemies, Satan has taken it very seriously. God does not make idle threats. Satan knew there was much to the words God speaks.

For some reason, God chose women to mete out His strategy against Satan. Women have been given a special assignment to be used of God against Satan. They are chosen vessels. Satan knows it, he is actually afraid of women.

God prophesied a time when the Seed of the woman was going to finally take care of Satan. Satan knew what God said was true. There was no way out for him. Satan knew woman had been destined to be a vehicle for his downfall. It was going to happen. The only question was when. The task was to stop woman from bearing seed.

Let us define the word *enmity*. According to the lexical aid to the Old Testament of the *Hebrew Greek Key Study Bible*, the word, *enmity* means "to be an enemy, to be hostile to, to treat as an enemy, to hate...." Basically it is a state of hostility. According to Webster's Dictionary, the definition is as follows: "enmity is the attitude or feelings of an enemy or enemies; hostility; antagonism."

Let us remember it was God who told Satan He was putting enmity between him and the woman. God did not tell Eve that he was putting enmity between her and the devil. He told Satan. God's words to Satan were a curse, a threat.

Though enmity was placed between Satan and the woman, that is not to say Satan is not also an enemy of man. As man is an ally of woman, Satan is also man's enemy. Now, the adversary has a mission to pursue. He now has the insurmountable task of making sure God's threats do not come to pass.

And with that motivation, Satan has put into operation a well thought out plan against women. It was essential for him to do something in order to save himself. Satan figured, "Well, if she is going to be my enemy, I'm not going to let her be the aggressor. I'll strike first, and then she'll always be on the defensive and maybe then she'll never succeed in fulfilling God's plan for her. If she never succeeds in fulfilling God's plan, I'll never be put out of commission." That's what he did. Until now, the deceiver has had a pretty good success rate.

Satan hates women

Let's take the lid off of a well-kept secret. The devil reserves a special hatred for women. We know he hates all mankind. But he has a particular animosity against women. That animosity that Satan has against women was placed there by God. Because he knows we are key to putting him out of business, he had come up with a special plan to keep us ignorant of our importance. We gain some insight into the adversary's hatred towards all women as we look at his reactions to the woman in Revelation 12:

> And when the dragon saw that he was cast unto the earth, he persecuted the woman which brought forth the man child. And to the woman were given two wings of a great eagle, that she might fly into the wilderness, into her place, where she is nourished for a time, and times, and half a time, from the face of the serpent . . . And the dragon was wroth with the woman, and went to make war with the remnant of her seed, which keep the commandments of God, and have the testimony of Jesus Christ. (Revelation 12:13-17)

A woman gives birth to a man child. After Satan is cast to the earth, he persecutes this woman. In verse 17, we read Satan was "wroth" with the woman. It is obvious the devil is angry at this woman, and wants revenge. The enmity placed between Satan and Eve was the beginning of an enmity between Satan and all women.

Satan wanted the son the woman was carrying. In Revelation 12:4, he stands before the woman to devour her child as soon as he is born. Satan does not like the fact women can have children. He hates our ability to reproduce.

When we do conceive, he will try to devour our children before they are born. After they are born, he will do all he can to make the children we have ineffective against him. He will use our children to cause us some of our greatest pain. If he does not succeed there, he will still persecute us as women just because we bring children into the world.

Why does Satan want our children? Every person born into the world is a potential overcomer for Christ. "And he that overcometh, and keepeth my works unto the end, to him will I give power over the nations. And he shall rule them with a rod of iron; as the vessels of a potter shall they be broken to shivers: even as I received of my Father" (Revelation 2: 26,27).

In Revelation 2:26,27 John the writer tells us that the overcomers will be given power to rule over the nations with a rod of iron. The man child the woman brings forth in Reverlation 12:5 is also to rule all nations with a rod of iron.

The Church, the woman in Revelation 12, and women in particular, have a responsibility to raise those who will overcome Satan by the blood of the Lamb and the word of their testimony (Revelation 12: 11). They will keep the commandments of God and will have the testimony of Jesus Christ. These are the overcomers.

Just as a woman influenced the first Adam to be independent of God, women have the mandate to influence their children and others to live lives dependent upon God.

It is very important to understand that Satan not only hates women, but he dislikes the authority they have over him. He fears the influence they can be for good in this world. This is the reason he has so cleverly woven his lies, erected barriers between the sexes, and sought to make women feel they are inferior.

The plan Satan has used against women in this world is very similar to the plan he has used against African Americans in this society: breaking spirits with the lie of inferiority. Satan is not very original. The deceiver has majored in telling us what we could not do or be.

Adam and Eve face consequences too

The consequences for the relationship between Adam and Eve were forecast in the curse placed on them. God foretold mutual frustration and many difficulties maintaining togetherness.

God did not design men to control women. God planned to be in complete control. When the first couple rebelled, He told them what was going to happen to both men and women without Him in control of their lives. The curse of sin was God telling Adam and Eve what it was going to be like in their relationship with each other as a result of their independence from Him.

It appears God's punishment for Adam was to let him experience exactly what God Himself had experienced. Adam rebelled against God's authority and took things into his own hands. Now Adam was going to get a taste of his own medicine. God was going to delegate him as head of the wife.

Adam would be the one with authority. Now he would get a chance to experience rebellion, lack of submission, disobedience, disrespect, and vying for control. According to the author of *Submission Is For Husbands, Too,* the word, *desire* used in the phase, "your desire shall be for your husband" has the connotation of trying to dominate another.

For Eve's part, she was told she would experience domination as Adam maintained the rule over her. This was part of the curse. Adam would become, not the servant-leader Jesus modeled, but a domineering tyrant.

So we see the relationship between men and women did not have a good start after the fall. Satan has capitalized on this fact with many tricks of his own. He actually was the cause of the curse. He brought the curse of independence from God upon the entire human race.

As long as there is division between the sexes, God's original plan for humankind to defeat the enemy could never be fulfilled.

Satan has tried to make sure togetherness would never reenter the earth's atmosphere. Satan's plan has been to put a permanent wedge between the sexes. Through domination, strife, control, jealousy, and contention, men and women have not been able to cooperate neither have they been able to together rule effectively over the earth. Divided, they have not been able to properly bring up godly seed, or most importantly, destroy the enemy and his works.

Women pay—even today . . .
Women become reactors to the pain inflicted upon them as a result of the curse. First, we have fought back in bitterness and anger. Second, we have become passive, accepting the lies of the enemy as truth. Third, we use a subtle method of control over others. By manipulating, intimidating, or threatening, women try to maintain a semblance of self-respect while pushing others to change.

The result: we as women are in bondage to ourselves. Instead of living the joyous life of bondservants to a God who cares about us, we blindly follow the path of the flesh and damage ourselves in the process.

. . . but they are of tremendous value to God
It is worth repeating, God did not make women inferior to men, but rather placed a special value on them. Even though it was part of the curse, on the positive side, God had a purpose for her being under her husband. It was for her protection. Since women have been given the mandate to be instrumental in Satan's downfall, they need special covering. God has covered her so that she could be preserved for such a time as this.

Imagine you owned a very expensive piece of crystal. Let's say that this piece of crystal was very valuable to you, not only because of its cost, but also because it first belonged to your great-grandmother. As a family heirloom, it becomes very important for you to keep this piece of crystal safe.

Now tell me, would you set this very valuable piece of crystal out on your coffee table or in the kids' toy box? No. You would put it up. You would probably keep it up in a cabinet. More than likely you would cover it to protect it. Valuable things are kept under cover. Valuable documents are kept in safe deposit boxes. Valuable paintings are kept in locked cases, sometimes with hired guards to protect them.

You are probably wondering what all this has to do with what we have been talking about. Well, women are very valuable to God. He has a plan for them and until the time of that plan, women have to be protected.

God knew with the advent of sin, selfishness and self-seeking would prevail and men and women would try to control each other. He knew rather than cooperation, rivalry, competition, jealous ambition, and all kinds of strife would be present.

The power of influence women had over men had to be brought under structured control. The plan for woman to be used to defeat the enemy had to be preserved. Thus the woman was placed under the man. It was not based on inferiority, less intelligence, or lesser standing on the part of women. To the contrary, she was valuable and as important to God as man was.

A woman is specially equipped with a sensitivity to walking in the Spirit. She has the God-given ability to defend her loved ones from the enemy. She is equipped with extra intuition to know when to pray for her children when they are in danger. She is given a special invitation to come into the throne room to ask God to reverse the damage of the enemy in the lives of her loved ones. There is so much she can do.

The truth

Women are extremely loved of God. They have tremendously important purposes to fulfill in our communities and this country. They have the potential to be powerful keys in the hand of God. African American women who learn about God's love and then commit themselves to loving others God's way can change things around for our communities and cities. Women, vessels chosen by God to revitalize our nation.

The truth will set women free. Oh, how the enemy hates the prospect of women realizing what Christ actually did when He liberated them by dying on the cross. Satan never wants us to find out that Christ can live inside us and that there is no distinction between male or female in the Spirit.

Satan knew that divided, the first couple would fall. He wanted man and woman divided in the garden of Eden, and he wants us to stay divided in spite of what Jesus accomplished at Calvary. Satan has purposely withheld from women the truth of who we can be in Christ. He has purposely attacked the position to which Christ has elevated us. Jesus Christ, the one and only true women's liberator!

Summary

Let's review some of the things we have said:

The Lord wanted the man and woman to become one flesh in order for them to learn unselfish love and also to reproduce more humans to serve Him. He wanted them to work together and thus be more than doubly effective than two individuals working separately. The enemy succeeded in putting a kink in God's plans, at least for a period of time.

Though the first man and woman were transferred out of the hands of God into the enemy's hand, God threatened Satan that woman would be used as an instrument of his destruction. Satan knows women are valuable in God's sight, so he has tried to get a head start with destructive attacks to the souls and spirits of women.

We'll see in the next chapter the old way is too costly for African American women. It's time to make a transfer back into the hands of God out from all of the plans of the enemy. Let us now take a closer look at how the the enemy's dual plans against women and against African Americans has resulted in a "double whammy" for African American women.

Chapter 5

Broken hearts—our biggest problem

The Lord is nigh unto them that are of a broken heart; and saveth such as be of a contrite spirit. **Psalm 34:18**

Satan knows the immense influence that godly African American women can have on tearing down his kingdom, so he has launched a doubly vicious attack against them. In doing so he has tried to stop everything God originally designed. The purpose of his attack is to prevent us from really knowing God's love.

Satan knows his fate is sealed when God takes hold of African American women and transfers them back into His hands. Satan has tried to stop us from getting back into God's hands. Satan has done it by lies, vicious lies about God, about ourselves, and about men. Satan has specifically targeted his attack at us. All of the actions of the enemy have been designed to circumvent the plan of God in our lives.

The enemy has set a destructive course for society's treatment of women. The devastating result is a broken heart. With a broken heart, a woman's emotions, mind, and will do not cooperate with one another. With a broken heart, a woman will often react to more pain and rejection.

Many African American women suffer from broken hearts. A woman with a broken heart will have a hidden rift with God and may believe He is responsible for her pain.

If a woman has had a poor relationship with her father or any authority figure, she will have a hard time trusting and maintaining a good relationship with her heavenly Father. She will often believe that God is unfair, doubt He has her best interests at heart, and not give Him her affection; though she may give Him her mind. Consequently, she will not reach her full potential in God until she is set free.

This is true even for women who are thought to be, or think of themselves as "good Christians."

A broken heart is woman's hidden problem.

Broken-hearted women are out of control. They have problems with explosive anger or depression, with appetites for food, drugs, or excitement. Some will turn to religious form and structure. Others tend to be perfectionists and make acceptance conditional upon performance. Many of these women have a form of godliness, but their very lives deny the power of God (2 Timothy 3:5).

It's even worse for "us"

Sisters of color, it's you the devil has fought the hardest to keep in bondage to fear, low self esteem, bitterness, and unforgiveness. The African American female must literally fight to keep from drowning under the negative feelings of rejection and inferiority.

Not only have men offended us, but racial prejudice has been an offense. We have many wounds inflicted upon us by the enemy. We've carried the scars of rejection all of our lives. Some of us were not wanted. Some of us were emotionally, physically and sexually abused. Wounds, rejection, and abuse break hearts.

Our hair has never been quite good enough. Our skin color or gender has kept us out of jobs or promotions and away from better grades. Our education was thought to be inferior.

Sometimes the men we married weren't able to get it together. Sometimes they haven't been able to provide for us. Some men have not even bothered to marry us. They make babies and leave us to care for them. Many of them take their anger at society out on us.

Some of our sons and daughters don't do well in school. Others are always getting into trouble. We did the best we knew how in raising them, yet some are in jail, some on drugs, some walking the streets, some living on the street, some in gangs, some not taking care of their families, and some with AIDS. That was not how we brought them up.

Yes, we live with fear, guilt, and condemnation. We harbor deep hurts and resentments. We have so much to be bitter about, and it is eating at us inside. These things drive us to alcohol, drugs, sex, food, and even to church. But we don't find lasting relief, because not even church can give the relief Jesus gives.

Some of us have learned to pull ourselves up in spite of everything. We have proved that we could make it. But not even success can ease the inner pain. Some of us have bought the myth of the independent Black woman who does not need any man. "It's time to get back at them, use them now. We'll be a success whether they care to come along or not. They've held us back too long. If they are too insecure, drunk, or fearful, we'll do it by ourselves."

Inside the shells of material or career success is a hurting, lonely little girl. The girl who may have compromised her conscience. The girl Jesus loves, accepts, and forgives, but does not really feel acceptable.

Jesus does not hold anything against us. Nothing grieves Him more than our indifference to Him. He's paid for our wrong, and He does not want us to continue to give ground to the enemy. He's even made His life available to us so we would not have to continue in our patterns of behavior. He's hurt when we don't accept what He's made available for us.

Satan's plan has worked. African American women have had a terrible weight of lies placed within our souls. We get confirmations of our "inferiority" from everywhere. The "proof" is hard to ignore.

Broken hearts lead to broken families

God's plan is for us to raise the next generation and lovingly influence others. But instead of wisdom and kindness on our lips, they contain sarcasm, gossip, slander, and criticism. Instead of being instruments of love, joy, and peace, we have become instruments of strife, anger, bitterness, jealousies, resentments, and unforgiveness.

The destructive attitudes that we end up with are helping Satan and his plan. Satan wants our seed. We are destroying ourselves, and we are being used as instruments in Satan's hands to bring further hurt and destruction to others. Instead of being tools in the hand of God for good, we are used by Satan for evil.

The end result is what Satan planned all along: broken families. Broken-hearted men and women usually end up separating, emotionally or physically. The wedge already existing between males and females is magnified when men and women have broken hearts.

As children sense even non-verbal strife and contention between men and women, it has a powerfully negative effect on them, an effect that is made worse by discipline done out of anger.

Children need our blessing, but are cursed instead. Parents have participated too often in passing on to children the very same curses that have been put on our race by others.

Do these phrases sound familiar? Chances are, you've heard them before. Hopefully, you've never used them:

"You're never going to amount to anything."

"Boy, you're just like your Daddy, the good for nothing low down dog."

"Girl, with your fast self, you're going to get pregnant just like your Aunt Bessie."

"I don't know what's wrong with you. You must be out of your mind."

Children of any color vitally need acceptance, kindness, encouragement, affection and instruction, among other things. Women with broken hearts who are trying to make marital relationships work do not always have the strength to give nurture, encouragement, and protection to their children.

Satan has been able to destroy whole generations because of his attacks against women.

Broken hearted women. Broken families. Troubled communities. Cities that need healing. Our entire nation needs healing.

There is hope . . .

There is one antidote to all that the enemy has done. There is one truth that when applied will erase all the enemy has done over years. The truth: God loves, values, and has a purpose for us. That truth came through Jesus.

If we could only get a true knowledge and understanding of God's love and care! If we as women could really experience that love for all it really is, the results would be dynamic! If that love could get beyond our intellectual knowledge and really sink into our being, we would never need to fear, feel insecure, or be bitter toward anyone.

How can we experience that love? We will need to be awakened to the truth. God will need to move among us and show us that love.

To those who are willing, God can reveal more and more of His sweet presence to us.

God has the power to break through what has happened from the beginning of time until now. He can do a "new thing" in us to refute all of the lies of the enemy. He can correct and bring back to original order what has taken the enemy thousands of years to distort.

As long as women continue to fall into the pattern the liar has set for us, we will continue to carry out his plan upon the earth. But if we can see behind the smoke screen to see exactly what is happening, we could learn to walk a different way. We could begin to cooperate with God's plan. We could become tools in God's hands.

Haven't you heard the good news? We've been set free by the blood of the Lamb. The emancipation proclamation has already been signed, Satan just didn't want us to know. Nothing he tells us is true. Now, we'll have to go through a deprogramming to get all of those false ideas and attitudes out of our system. We'll need to wipe everything out of our emotions and start over with a clean slate.

We especially need to put a lot of our religious training on the line. The Bible is the book the enemy loves to quote to give credibility to his lies. He does not interpret very well, but does not mind using sincere men, even those whom God has called, to peddle his lies. God will help us sort the truth from the error.

It's time we put our spiritual armor on and fight the real war (Ephesians 6:10-17). It's time we took up our spiritual weapons and win a few battles. It's time we put ourselves under God's authority. It's time we become weapons in the hand of God. It's time we demonstrated the victory secured at the cross (Colossians 2:15).

Our responsibility

There is plenty of blame to go around. We have all made wrong choices, not obeyed God's Word, and been ignorant of truth. We have often not known how to get out of the destructive cycles. Satan's plans have succeeded to some degree.

With truth, we are responsible to put a stop to all the enemy has done in our homes and communities. If we choose to let it continue, we will only have ourselves to blame.

Though we have spent a lot of time talking about what has been done to us by others, by no means do we want to imply that women have no responsibility for themselves and those whom God puts in their lives.

We have played our part in falling into and staying in the traps of the enemy. We have played a part in keeping others in spiritual prisons. It's not that we have done anything out of the ordinary. Our responses have been natural responses. But Christians are without excuse. We have the resources to respond above the natural.

Our contribution to the destructive cycle has been letting the pain of rejection control our reactions towards others. We have also lost love and respect for men. Since many men, especially husbands, are in positions of authority in our lives, respect on our part is very important. The lack of respect that we have for men carries over to God.

We must turn from these ways. As we realize brokenness in our hearts, we can ask God to put our heart back together. He heals the broken in heart (Psalm 14:3).

Things we have to settle
We will have to take responsibility for our wrongs. We will have to admit them. We cannot cover our own sin (Proverbs 28:13). We will have to take responsibility for our part before we can expect God to come to our defense.

We will have to forgive. When we forgive, God gives us the power to go even further. *He can help us bring life to those who have offended us.*

We've actually blocked God's love, acceptance and forgiveness from getting through to others by our attitudes and behavior. We may be the only Jesus some will ever see. What kind of Jesus do we portray — an angry, bitter, proud Jesus? That's a false image. That's not Jesus. That's our flesh.

Jesus is meek, lowly, humble. He knows how to be angry, but He does not sin. He does not hold it in.

There is good news! God promises to heal the broken in heart (Psalm 147:3). God says He is near the broken hearted (Psalm 34:18). There is tremendous hope for African American women. Let us fall on our faces before God, get our broken hearts bound up, and receive a touch of new life. We can then be used of God to bring healing to others.

God is putting many broken hearts back together again. Many of us are going through tremendous pain and struggles in our lives because God is doing open heart surgery on us. He is melting the bitterness. We have to submit no matter how painful it is.

The pain does not last forever. We may need to shed tears. It is part of the healing process. We do not want our heart condition to get worse. We must not let the pain force us off the operating table in the middle of open heart surgery. Broken hearts can be healed. We must settle in our hearts we will go through the healing process.

So let us forget what is behind us and let us press on. Forget it— forget the good and the bad. This is a new day, a new beginning. The failures, the pain, and the hurts of yesterday are under the blood of Jesus.

There will be times the Holy Spirit will take us to the past to undo some hooks, to release some people, and to even forgive ourselves; but for right now, let's just forget the past. We could never figure it out anyway. Let's just go with a clean slate to learn a "new thing."

Summary

Let's review the vicious cycle the enemy has kept going in this world. He hates humans. He has especially targeted his hatred against African American women.

By using others to abuse us, he has caused brokenness in the seat of our emotions and affections. That has caused us to be cold-hearted and hard-hearted. This has made it difficult for African American women to trust men, nurture children and carry out God's purposes of training, influencing, and cooperating with others.

It's time this whole cycle stopped. African American women can put a stop to it. But we can only stop it if we are willing to live in the realm of the Spirit. It is in this realm we can regain our original purpose and be an instrument in God's hand to bruise the enemy's head. It's in this realm we can reverse the curse of the devil.

Many would have us believe change only comes from elsewhere. Some would have us think when drug dealers, abortionists, and gang members change, things will get better for our cities. The next chapter refutes those ideas and tells us where real change must begin.

Chapter 6

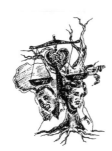

Balancing the scales

For it is time for judgment to begin with the family of God; and if it begins with us, what will the outcome be for those who do not obey the gospel of God?
Peter 4:17 NIV

Because of the pivotal role women have in homes, churches, and communities, broken-hearted women lead to a nation in crisis. We as a nation are under judgment.

Individuals have lost hope. Many are on the brink of despair. Our families need to be redeemed from strife and division. Our cities need to be rescued from the clutches of evil. Our nation needs healing.

God is able to heal our nation. There is nothing impossible with God. God's people have resources necessary to win the spiritual battles raging in our cities.

How do we get God's attention? How do we get an audience with God? And how do we get Him to heal our land?

Judgment can be averted three different ways. *The first way is for righteousness to outweigh unrighteousness.* As long as there is a remnant of righteous people, a nation is exalted (Proverbs 14:34). And it does not take a lot of righteous people to spare a nation.

Repentance of a community of people is the second way to avert judgment. God always gives us plenty of warning when He is ready to mete out judgment. He sends His servants to tell us that our time is running out and encourages us to repent. Repentance is when people humble themselves, pray for mercy, seek God, and turn from their sin.

The third way to avert judgment is for someone who has an audience with God to ask God for mercy instead of judgment. God desires to give mercy so much, He actually seeks people (intercessors) who will ask Him for mercy. This is often the plan that is put into action when people do not listen to the message of repentance from God's servants.

Sodom & Gomorrah: righteousness and intercession

The first example is taken from the book of Genesis. In chapter 18, we see Abraham functioning as an intercessor for the cities of Sodom and Gomorrah. The sin of Sodom and Gomorrah was "very grievous," and because of the sin; the judgment God passed was destruction.

Abraham went to the Lord to intercede for the city. He actually bargained with God. "If there are fifty righteous people, will you spare the city? What about forty? Twenty? Ten?" As they continued to dialogue, God agreed to spare the city if only ten righteous people were found.

This account ends on a sad note. Sodom and Gomorrah were not spared. Ten righteous people were not found. However, God did spare four people by bringing them out of the city before the destruction. Some speculate if Abraham had gone down to four, God might have even spared it upon His request.

That may be true. We know God will listen to His children. God wants to answer prayer. Many things are not done because God's people do not ask. "Ye lust, and have not: ye kill, and desire to have, and cannot obtain: ye fight and war, yet ye have not, because ye ask not" (James 4:2).

Nineveh: The way of repentance

The second place to look is in the book of Jonah. In Jonah 1:2, we see Jonah was to cry against wickedness and pronounce judgment against the city of Nineveh. He got sidetracked,but in Jonah 3:4, he cried out the following: "Yet forty days, and Ninevah shall be overthrown."

Forty days came and went. No judgment came from God.

What happened? The people of Ninevah believed the Word of God, fasted, and repented. Actually, they followed the command of their king. He proclaimed a fast and told all of the people to be covered with sackcloth, cry mightily unto God, and turn away from their evil and violent ways.

Because the people repented (turned), God repented from the evil He had said he would do (Jonah 3:10).

Repentance is powerful. Repentance and intercession are unbeatable.

How do the cities in America weigh in?

In the case of Nineveh, judgment was averted. The proper conditions were met. What would it be in the cases of Detroit or Chicago? How would Atlanta, New York, Los Angeles, and San Francisco fare?

When God weighs these cities will He find more sin on the part of the unrighteous or more righteousness on the part of His people? What is the destiny of these cities? Is it possible for things to change?

One might say, "Well, we don't have a problem. I'm sure the city I live in will certainly find favor with God. I'm sure the enemy will not be allowed to bring destruction here. We have churches on every corner. We've got the religious people. Most of the people I know go to church."

"Wait a minute. Did you say religious people or righteous people?"

"Well, now I don't know. I'm not so sure. I can show you a lot of churches where people speak in tongues, or have Bible verses memorized, or pack the folks in on Sunday. Certainly, these should count for something!"

If we follow the set conditions, we have much hope for change. Proverbs 14:34 tells us righteousness exalts a nation, but sin is a reproach to any people. One of the words that describes the Hebrew word from which righteousness comes from is 'cleansed.'

The church is "America's Only Hope," to borrow a phrase from Dr. Anthony Evans in his book of the same name. And prayer is the church's only hope. As the people of God turn to God in prayer, they will be cleansed so that the light will shine forth in the midst of the darkness.

Massive judgment has been averted in this nation because of the righteousness of the people of God and the prayers offered up in the past. But we would hate to wake up one morning and find out that the scales have been tipped. We have been spared much, but how much longer do we have before the sin outweighs the righteousness? From all indications there is not much time left.

No doubt God has blessed America. In spite of all of the wrongs we discussed, much good has come from this nation. But blessing time is running out. The enemy has increased evil faster than God's people have increased righteousness.

The choice: reducing sin or increasing righteousness

In many cases, Christians get upset with expressions of sins such as drug addiction, abortion, or homosexuality. We all have probably gotten mail from well-meaning organizations whose focus is to reduce the number of people involved in these kinds of activities. But how much mail comes from organizations who want to increase the righteousness among those who have decided to follow Jesus?

If we look at the scales of sin and righteousness, there are two choices. We can either increase righteousness or we can decrease sin. If we maintain the same level of righteousness and somehow get sinners to stop sinning, the scales will tip to righteousness.

But decreasing sin must not be the only approach. It has some serious limitations. For one, we are trying to tell people to turn from their ways without the power of the Holy Spirit in their lives. That's unfair.

The other problem? Those who follow the "reducing sin" approach have little personal involvement in the lives of those against whom they protest. The perception on the outside goes something like this: "You don't really care about me as a person. All you see is what I do."

Turning the lights back on is a better way

It is much better to increase righteousness among the righteous. That will do two things. First, it will decrease sin among our own ranks. This will lower the effects of sin and also increase the effects of righteousness.

Second, it will bring light to those who are in darkness. People living in darkness are always drawn to the light. Our saltiness will make them thirsty, and many will come to the water to drink of the fountain of life, Jesus Christ.

Have you ever come home to a dark house, turned functioning lights on, and the darkness overcame the light? No. Darkness always disappears when lights are on. It will happen in our cities when Jesus begins to shine through God's people.

We have clear instructions from the Word of God how this happens. Again, prayer is the key. Prayer will tilt the scales and give us more time to reach the lost.

So far, everything has been pointing us back to prayer. We have said prayer is a key to the Church's effectiveness and will avert certain judgment. Prayer is the key to saving our cities.

But how do we make a "prayer movement" happen? Should we get more people to come to prayer services? Should we call more national days of prayer?

That certainly would not hurt. But Scripture tells us the power of prayer is not found in numbers. If the number of people praying was the answer, we would have had the largest revival in the history of this country when over 300,000 people descended on Washington, D.C. to pray a few years ago.

Righteousness is the starting place

Romans 6:13 says, "Neither yield ye your members as instruments of unrighteousness unto sin: but yield yourselves unto God, as those that are alive from the dead, and your members as instruments of righteousness unto God."

There are many sins of the body that need to be taken into account. There are sins of the mind and tongue. They are the sins that got Israel into trouble, and the same ones keeping us in trouble. Our families are being broken up by sins of the tongue. Churches are broken by the destructive use of the tongue. Children's hearts are broken by the wrong use of the tongue.

Let us be honest and evaluate our lives under the microscope of the Word of God. In whose hand are you a tool? Are you used by God sometimes and by Satan at other times? A mixture indicates double-mindedness and instability (James 1:8).

Prayerfully consider the two categories on the next page and determine which you find yourself in most of the time. Are you a 'Christian' who is being used by the enemy more than by God?

In whose hand are you a tool?
God's Hand:
- listens, prays, instructs, restores.

- thoughts/words of kindness, comfort, encouragement, exhortation, forgiveness, mercy, blessing, acceptance, and seasoned with grace.

- tries to help other change direction; gently confronts, rebukes and warns as needed, but only out of love and concern for the other person's well-being; done under the direction of the Holy Spirit, out of humility; often accompanied by fasting.

Satan's Hand:
- thoughts/words of criticism, condemnation, judgmentalism, bitterness, resentments, unforgiveness, anger, harshness, wrath and impatience.

- uses silent treatment, withholds affection, withdraws or talks a lot without listening to others well, lashes out in anger, gossips, slanders.

- prayerlessness, or use of manipulative prayers.

- always tries to correct or change others; corrects out of anger, harshly, without prayer and fasting and with an attitude of superiority.

The prayer recipe
2 Chronicles 7:14 says, "If my people, which are called by my name, shall humble themselves, and pray, and seek my face, and turn from their wicked ways; then will I hear from heaven, and will forgive their sin, and will heal their land."

The responsibility of the healing of our land belongs to the people of God. It has four components. They are 1) humble yourself, 2) pray, (3) seek God's face and (4) turn from your wicked ways.

When people talk about this verse, they often refer to or emphasize just one or two ingredients in this four-part recipe. In fact, literature from a national prayer organization quoted this verse listing only three out of the four.

Most people know when it takes four ingredients to make a dish, trying to get by with just two or three does not work. If a cake recipe on the back of a Bisquick® box calls for eggs, milk, sugar, and Bisquick® mix, using less than all four will not result in the cake. Eggs and milk make a scrambled egg mixture. The flour mixture and milk might make biscuits. Sugar, milk and eggs might make egg nog. But none of these is the cake we wanted to make. In order to make the cake, we need to put in all four ingredients.

In order to heal our land, we need to follow the instructions given. If our land is not healed, then those responsible for the "cooking"— the people of God—are at fault.

Can someone explain why Mr. and Mrs. My People are out of the kitchen, down the street telling Mr. and Mrs. Not My People what to do to bring healing to this land?

It's a little confusing. Perhaps we should get back into the kitchen. Maybe a few of us can get started on making this cake. Who knows? Others might join us!

Each one of these components listed in 2 Chronicles 7:14 requires action. It looks as if there might be a little work involved.

Someone might say, "You mean I just can't pray? I've got to humble myself too? What do you mean turn from my wicked ways? I don't have any wicked ways. Why, I read my Bible every day. I have read it all the way through twelve times. I go to church three times a week. I am surely not like those wicked homosexuals and those money hungry abortionists. They are the ones bringing our land to ruin! If we could just get them to stop all of their sinning, we would not be in the mess we're in. Sign me up for the next march!"

American Christianity is full of activity. There are plenty of petitions to sign, letters to write, demonstrations to attend, and causes to support. If one is looking for action, look no further. Perhaps there is some merit to this kind of activity. But much of it only serves to misdirect our focus. It makes us forget our kitchen duties. It numbs us to our own responsibility.

Prayer will increase righteousness

If we pray the prayers of the prayer recipe, we will become the persons of prayer that actually have an audience with God. As we get more answers to prayers, we will pray more. As a result, we will begin to see more right living.

As African American women learn the prayers of the prayer recipe, God can teach us to possess the land of our families and our communities. We can be the vessels God will use to heal the broken hearts of many, bring deliverance, set at liberty them that are bruised, and give sight to the blind. Yes, God can make us weapons of love and light to send us into enemy territory and bring freedom to many.

Summary

Let us accept our responsibility to increase righteousness. Let us stop looking to the government and others to bring change to this land. If we would lay our lives down in prayer, righteousness can be increased.

We could see change if we had a few more living righteous lives. We could see change everywhere if God's people followed the recipe.

It is easier to blame others for the ills of our society than to accept the truth about our own failures. Maybe we need to sing this song: "It's not the homosexual, it's not the abortionist or the crack dealer, but it's me oh, Lord, standing in the need of prayer. . . ."

The next section of the book will explore the journey to wholeness. God has already initiated this process in many African American women. Perhaps it has already begun in your life as well. It's a journey into the presence of God.

God's presence will reverse the enemy's work in our lives. His presence will give us back the ability to fulfill the original plan of destroying the works of the enemy and bring hope to our homes and communities. Becoming a house of prayer instead of a den of thieves will result from God's presence in our lives.

Prayer is a key to healing broken hearts. Prayer is a key to healing our land. In the next section, we will look at the ingredients in the prayer recipe: humbling, praying, seeking, and turning. To admit our responsibility would be humbling. Humbling ourselves, the first ingredient of the prayer recipe, is where we must begin and is the focus of the next chapter.

Section two: Healing process

Chapter 7

Humble

Humble yourselves therefore under the mighty hand of God, that he may exalt you in due time. **1 Peter 5:6.**

Esohe! Come here right now and put this mayonnaise back up in the refrigerator. Why don't you *ever* put things back up? If I've told you once, I've told you a *million* times, put the food you use back up when you finish with it"!

"I didn't leave it out, Mommy."

"What! You think it walked out of the refrigerator by itself"?

Holy Spirit conviction: exaggeration—damaging a child's spirit—sarcasm—false accusation—excessive anger. "Lord, I was wrong. Forgive me."

"Listen, Esohe, I'm sorry I yelled at you this morning over the mayonnaise. After I thought about it, the Lord reminded me that *I* left it out. Please forgive me for blaming you and fussing so. I was wrong."

It's humbling enough to admit it to ourselves when we are wrong. To apologize to others is even more so. To apologize to your own children is not pleasant. Some people have the idea that children, students, employees (anyone under us) do not need an apology from us when we are wrong. I had the same idea until the first time God told me to apolgize to my children for allowing my anger to get out of control. That was *one* way of dealing with the pride in my life.

We have the same problem admiting our wrong to God. It's just so hard to humble ourselves before God and admit we are the ones at fault for a lot of things the enemy has done in our lives, our family members, and even our cities.

The first step in humbling ourselves is confession, which means simply to agree with God. We need to agree with God where we have been wrong. Confession will lead to a change in our attitude of pride.

"But what do I confess? What have I done to contribute to the problems of our society?"

Many people honestly do not know what part they have played in society's ills. But we must at least agree to agree with God if He can show us.

The importance of admitting our sins

Sin gives an open invitation to evil spirits to work in our lives. It allows them to work in the circumstances of our lives. It gives them the legal right to block the blessings of God. Just as a parent does not desire for their children to be bullied, even if his child asked for it, God does not like Satan beating up on His children.

As Christians, we are covered by the blood of Jesus Christ. As long as we stay hid in Christ, no matter our personal shortcomings, the enemy cannot get through to us. But when we step out of Christ, by acting carnally, it is like painting ourselves with fluorescent paint that attracts the attention of tormenting spirits.

If we confess, admit the sin, we get right back under the blood and are cleansed from all unrighteousness (1 John 1:9). We are really not any better than we were. The only difference is that we are not living out of our own abilities.

Hiding in Christ, we constantly depend upon the grace and power of God for righteous living. As we confess our faults, we are reminded that in our flesh is no good thing and that Christ is our righteousness (Romans 7:18; 1Corinthians 1:30).

How do we know what to confess?

The word of God says we have not because we ask not (James 3:2). To find out if we have contributed to the problem, we need to ask God to open our eyes and show us. He said he would answer any prayer in line with His will. We know He desires us to have our eyes opened to truth (Luke 4:18 and 2 Corinthians 4:4). The first prayer in our journey is to ask for help to see the things we need to confess.

David gives us an excellent example of this kind of prayer in Psalm 139:23, 24. He says, "Search me, O God, and know my heart: try me, and know my thoughts: And see if there be any wicked way in me, and lead me in the way everlasting." We'll call this the *searchlight prayer.*

The searchlight prayer is desperately needed. It is an essential first prayer, truly a part of the humbling process. The psalmist tells us if we regard iniquity in our hearts, God will not hear us (Psalm 66:18). The keystone of all prayer is for God to hear us. If He does not hear us, there is no possibility of a response.

The searchlight prayer is very important because we do not know our own hearts. The prophet in Jeremiah 17:9 says, "The heart is deceitful above all things and desperately wicked: who can know it?" Only God knows our hearts (Psalm 44:21). David asks God to try his heart in Psalm 26:2. It is very possible to be deceived about our own righteousness, which is to God nothing but filthy rags (Isaiah 64:6).

Some possible surprises

Judgment begins in the household of faith. If we were to get the Judge's verdict, we might find we have been weighed in at the scales and found wanting. It's important to get God's verdict on our lives and not someone else's word for it.

As we go to the Judge, it is possible some of us who think we're on our way to heaven may find out that we've never really asked Jesus into our lives with our hearts. Oh, we've done so with our lips, but when He came to take us up on the invitation, we said "Not now!" Some of us who think we are Christians are not.

A relationship, a habit, or a self-appointed right to be bitter may have been the reason for the hesitation. After all we're human and we need a little affection, a little fun in life. We can't bring ourselves to give it all up.

God does not ask us to change before He comes in, but He does ask us to surrender all to Him and allow Him to make changes according to what He knows is best.

Others of us may find garbage in a closet. Jesus has done a work of house cleaning in our lives and removed garbage out of the house. Why then would we rummage through the garbage later? We say, "It's so hard to let go of bitterness and resentment. Let's just keep it back in the closet. Who knows? I might need it someday."

Rejoicing is in order for all who get a clean bill of spiritual health. We need healthy people. Even healthy people will be able to do the work of God with new confidence. Voluntary examinations are always better than being forced to seek attention.

How to agree with the findings

When individuals turn themselves in to the Chief Physician for a spiritual check-up and get a surprise in their report; the same Physician will be able to fix it. We only need to be willing to admit (confess) when we get our test results. Look at the following:

To some who were confident of their own righteousness and looked down on everybody else, Jesus told this parable: "Two men went up to the temple to pray, one a Pharisee and the other a tax collector. The Pharisee stood up and prayed about himself: 'God, I thank you that I am not like other men—robbers, evildoers, adulterers—or even like this tax collector. I fast twice a week and give a tenth of all I get.' "But the tax collector stood at a distance. He would not even look up to heaven, but beat his breast and said, 'God, have mercy on me, a sinner.' "I tell you that this man, rather than the other, went home justified before God. For everyone who exalts himself will be humbled, and he who humbles himself will be exalted." (Luke 18:9-14 NIV)

We all would do well to imitate the publican rather than the pharisee in our prayers and attitudes. The publican asked for mercy for himself while the pharisee was busy comparing himself with the sinner; he came out ahead in his own eyes. Sometimes our eyes are the only eyes in which we come out ahead. We can be so deceived about our own "good," it is pathetic. God's evaluation is essential.

Yes, it can be humbling to find out some surprises that were buried, but humbling is the point of the first ingredient. However, that won't be the end. As the last part of verse 14 in the passage in Luke indicates, "for every one that exalts himself shall be abased, and every one that humbles himself shall be exalted."

After God shows us our real heart, we agree He is correct. This is the *prayer of confession*. As already stated, confession simply means agreeing with God. We then ask Him for mercy since His mercies are manifold (Nehemiah 9:19). We also know He is faithful and just to forgive us our sin and to cleanse us from all unrighteousness (1 John 1:9). By faith, we then ask Him to clothe us in the righteousness of His Son (Philippians 3:9 and 1 Corinthians 1:30).

In humbling ourselves we may have to admit wrong to others, sometimes to those we have offended. Other times we confess to members of the body of Christ as we share our faults with them in small fellowship groups. We will experience healing as others pray for us (James 5:16). Knowing our faults will also serve to keep us out of pride when God does have mercy on us and uses us. We'll know it was Him and not us.

The difficulty of these prayers

We have discussed two types of prayers that are not often heard in most prayer meetings: the searchlight prayer and prayer of confession. They are components of the humbling process.

There are many obstacles to these first two prayers. They look simple on paper, but in reality are very hard. Pride has a tremendous stronghold on most lives. It is very subtle. Pride keeps us from admitting there is anything wrong or makes excuses for obvious wrongs. We will have to call upon God often to be able to make it through the process of humility.

Denying, blaming, or rationalizing are not compatible with humility. These are the things that we have to watch. It is almost certain all of us will try to get away with some of these defense mechanisms from time to time. But we must not tolerate them.

Fasting can help us to humble ourselves. David tells us in Psalm 35:13 that he humbled his soul with fasting. Fasting often accompanied confession of sin (Daniel 9:3; 1 Samuel 7:6; Nehemiah 9:1,2).

Isaiah 58:6,7 tells us about the fast that God has chosen. It is a fast to loose the bands of wickedness, to undo the heavy burdens, and to let the oppressed go free and break every yoke. Fasting is a must for those who would be burdened to pray for the healing of our land.

First, we need to fast for ourselves. We are explicitly told by Joel to sanctify a fast and to call a solemn assembly (Joel 1:14, 2:12-15).

A person's health condition may preclude the advisability of fasting. If you have never fasted before, you should begin slowly. Seek a physician's counsel before embarking on any extended fast.

Although fasting can be done religiously and with pride by some (like the publican in Luke 18), that should not deter others from being obedient to God in this area. For more detailed information on the subject of fasting, the book *God's Chosen Fast* by Arthur Wallis is recommended.

Casting our cares upon the Lord

We have looked at the aspect of humbling ourselves in three different ways; the searchlight prayer, prayer of confession, and fasting.

The next prayer is the *casting prayer*. In this prayer we give or cast all of our worries, cares, anxieties, concerns, and burdens over to the Lord.

The Lord tells us in Matthew 11:30 that His yoke is easy and His burden is light. He also tells us in verses 28 and 29 to "Come unto me all ye that labour and are heavy laden, and I will give you rest. Take my yoke upon you, and learn of me; for I am meek and lowly in heart: and ye shall find rest unto your souls."

Worries and cares are an expenditure of much time and energy thinking about an issue. We fret about these issues over and over without coming to any conclusions and find ourselves going around in circles. According to Scripture, this is wrong. It signifies a lack of trust.

But it is unrealistic to suggest we should pretend nothing concerns us. In the casting prayer, we give our concerns to the Lord, fully assured that He is able to care for us. We leave them there, and refuse to pick them back up by constantly trying to figure them out, or falling back into old thinking habits.

What does casting our cares on God have to do with humility? In 1 Peter 5:7, we are told, "Casting all your care upon him; for he careth for you." Just before that, Peter says in verses 5 and 6, "Be clothed with humility; for God resisteth the proud, and giveth grace to the humble. Humble yourselves therefore under the mighty hand of God, that He may exalt you in due time."

Ideally, we should give our concerns to the Lord and wait on the Lord to work them out. But we humans have the tendency to take back what we give the Lord. When we refuse to let God have our burdens, we're saying that we know more than He does. It is indeed one of the biggest evidences of pride in our lives.

Anytime we worry again about the thing we have committed to the Lord, we have taken it back. Now that does not mean that a thought can never cross our mind. That may happen. However, that's when we say to ourselves and any one else, "That's not my problem anymore. Someone else is handling that." Then we let it go. If we need to, we go back to God and remind Him that we chose to let that particular concern stay with Him. But if God convicts us we have already taken something back, again we agree with His verdict of sin. We thank Him for His forgiveness and cleansing, ask Him for help to leave it in His hands, and we recommit it to the Lord.

We may have to do this over and over again before we allow it to stay in His hands any length of time. Having to admit the inability to keep things in God's hands is humbling. Thank God that we can confess our sin as many times as it takes.

The casting prayer brings peace
When we truly cast all of our cares and concern over to God, the result should be peace of mind. This prayer is dependent on a trust in God's faithfulness in the midst of adverse circumstances.

Paul states in Philippians 4:11,12 that he had learned to be content in whatever state he found himself. He knew both how to be abased (having nothing) and how to abound (having all things). God desires us to be unwavering in our confidence in Him in spite of our circumstances.

In this life, we will have trials. We will have to go through many fires and rivers, but God's Word promises He will be with us. "When thou passest through the waters, I will be with thee; and through the rivers, they shall not overflow thee: when thou walkest through the fire, thou shall not be burned; neither shall the flame kindle upon thee" (Isaiah 43:2).

Scriptural examples of humility

The Scriptures give us many examples of those who knew their God and had learned to cast their cares on Him. Most of our lives pale in comparison. The apostles in Acts 5 show us one example. In verses 40 and 41, after they were beaten, they left rejoicing that they were counted worthy to suffer shame for Jesus' name.

We see entirely different attitudes today. How many of us would do that? We would be going to the nearest lawyer to slap our persecutors with a lawsuit. It will be a glorious day when we are able by God's grace to jump for joy when people persecute or say all kinds of evil against us falsely for the sake of Jesus instead of always trying to defend ourselves.

There are a few things we can learn from the three Hebrew boys who were thrown in the fiery furnace. Daniel 3:17-18 quotes them as saying:"If it be so, our God whom we serve is able to deliver us from the furnace of blazing fire; and He will deliver us out of your hand, O king. But even if He does not, let it be known to you, O king, that we are not going to serve your gods or worship the golden image that you have set up."

The three young men were confident in the ability of their God to deliver. They also had an attitude of humility before God. In faith they declared God would deliver them, but they wanted the king to know that even if He would not deliver, they would still not serve his gods.

That was a humble attitude. They knew God could deliver them and believed He would deliver them, but refused to have the arrogance to demand that God deliver them. Much like the apostles in Acts 5, they were willing and ready to suffer for their faith even if it meant death.

The people referred to in both of the examples given above had one thing in common: they knew God. When we don't fully know God, we become fearful, worried, and frustrated when things go wrong. It is impossible to look at our circumstances correctly; that is, from God's point of view, without an in-depth knowledge of Him. Daniel 11:32 NAS says, "The people who know their God will display strength and take action."

Summary

We are exhorted many times in Scripture to "humble ourselves." Many times we skip that requirement because it is painful to humble ourselves. We must remember that humbling ourselves is the first ingredient to effective prayer.

Three kinds of prayers are necessary to the humbling process: searchlight, casting, and confession.

Maybe if we begin with the biblical recipe, we'll find the crack houses and the abortion clinics closing because of a lack of customers. Similar things have happened before. Perhaps, if we would take the admonition to humble ourselves as seriously as we do our marching and petitioning, we could see more of God's agenda fulfilled.

African American women, we can humble ourselves and admit we are not really good representatives of Jesus' life.

Questions for thought and action

1. Have you ever sought the Father about your possible contribution in the problems of your family, neighborhood, and church? _____YES _____NO

2. Have you ever prepared for communion with fasting in order to hear clearly from God?_____YES _____NO

3. When someone points out a fault of yours, do you find it difficult to be nice to the person?_____SOMETIMES _____ALWAYS _____SELDOM _____ALMOST NEVER

4. How did you react in the last major financial or relationship trial in your life? Did you worry or were you able to leave your cares in God's hand?

5. List three concrete things that you will do to humble yourself.

_____
_____
_____
_____

Chapter 8

Pray

Is any among you afflicted? let him pray. Is any merry? let him sing psalms. Is any sick among you? let him call for the elders of the church; and let them pray over him, anointing him with oil in the name of the Lord. And the prayer of faith shall save the sick, and the Lord shall raise him up; and if he has committed sins, they shall be forgiven him. Confess your faults one to another and pray one for another that you may be healed. The effectual fervent prayer of a righteous man availeth much. **James 5:13-16**

The next ingredient in the recipe is prayer. After we have humbled ourselves, we are ready to bring our petitions to God. We have already been praying as we have gone to God to ask Him to search us and have agreed with the things He has revealed to us. Now what petitions should we pray? Petitions are *asking prayers.*

We should ask God for things clearly consistent with the promises of God. However, we should not just pull a verse out of the air and think it is sufficient. Even if we have a promise from Scripture, we need to be sure that the promise is appropriate for us. We must rightly divide the Word of God, and not just make it say what we want it to say (2 Timothy 2:15).

The author of James 4:3 tells us that we ask and receive not because we ask amiss; that is, we ask with wrong motives in order to fulfill our own fleshly desires.

The key to answered prayer

Is it really possible to go to God with the confidence He will answer our prayers? Imagine the power we would have for bringing change to our cities if God answered whatever we asked.

Many times Scripture promises to answer prayer. Let's look at some of those promises:

> And whatsoever ye shall ask in my name, that I will do, that the Father may be glorified in the Son. If ye shall ask any thing in my name, I will do it. (John 14:13,14)

> If ye abide in me and my words abide in you, ye shall ask what ye will, and it shall be done unto you. (John 15:7)

> Beloved, if our heart condemn us not, then have we confidence toward God. And whatsoever we ask, we receive of him, because we keep his commandments, and do those things that are pleasing in his sight. And this is his commandment, That we should believe on the name of his Son Jesus Christ, and love one another, as he gave us commandment. (1 John 3:21-23)

> And this is the confidence that we have in him, that, if we ask any thing according to his will, he heareth us: And if we know that he hear us, whatsoever we ask, we know that we have the petitions that we desired of him. (1 John 5: 14,15)

Yes, everything we ask can be answered. We should not be satisfied with "yes", "no" and "maybe" answers. The key is growing close to Him so we pray the prayers He wants to answer "yes." That goal might take a long time to obtain, yet it should be our goal.

To be able to receive whatever we ask of God has nothing to do with God's ability to answer. It has to do with us. It happens when we have confidence towards God. We have confidence towards God when we obey His commandments. We are told specifically which command is most important. It's the love command.

Love is the key to answered prayer.

If we are doing things pleasing to Him, we love one another. As He is in us and as we are in Him, we only ask those things that He wants in the first place. In this way, He answers all of our prayers.

If love is the key, what is love? God's love is different from the way we love. We love with conditions, but God puts no conditions on love. (There are conditions to receive God's favor, friendship and blessings, but not His love because when we were yet sinners Christ died for us). If we want to love the same way God loves, we have to love without conditions. This unconditional love of God is already in us if we are Christians. That love is described in 1 Corinthians 13:4-7.

> Love endures long and is patient and kind; love never is envious nor boils over with jealousy; is not boastful or vainglorious, does not display itself haughtily. It is not conceited—arrogant and inflated with pride; it is not rude (unmannerly), and does not insist on its own right or its own way, for it is not self-seeking; it is not touchy or fretful or resentful; it takes no account of the evil done to it—pays no attention to a suffered wrong. It does not rejoice at injustice and unrighteousness, but rejoices when right and truth prevail. Love bears up under anything and everything that comes, is ever ready to believe the best of every person, its hopes are fadeless under all circumstances and it endures everything (without weakening). AMPLIFIED

Why is God's love not seen through His people?

God is love. His very character and life is unconditional love. The world desperately needs to see that love. This love dwells in the believer's spirit.

How is it that people can't see it?

Each of us is like individual "TV channels" to transmit God's love and presence to our world. Our signals can make for a cloudy or clear transmission.

The problem is not God's love. Our soul determines whether God's love will be clearly transmitted to others. The soul is the middle man. It stands between the spirit and the body. Bitterness, unforgiveness, or fears tied up in our soul block God's love from flowing through us. The Holy Spirit has to overcome attitudes in our minds, desires and emotions to get through to our behavior and responses. What is in our spirit can then be demonstrated to the world.

Though the love is there in our spirit, there may be situations or people that make it hard for us to respond with God's unconditional love. Past experience may have instilled patterns of defensive emotional responses, negative thinking, and selfish desires or expectations.

Essentially, what we are saying is we have to decide whether we want to take the risk of being transparent. Will we allow God's Word to change our negative thinking? Will we allow the Holy Spirit to comfort (heal) our emotional hurts? Will we forgive others of unloving actions and attitudes they have inflicted upon us?

It's up to us to unclog the signals. We determine the clarity and clear transmission of our "channel" of blessing.

God's Spirit is ready to flow. He will help us put away the flesh, continue to fill us with His presence, and make His love real to us.

God's priority in prayer

Sometimes when we pray, we want God to change the person or situation. That is not God's priority. God wants to change us more than He wants to change our situation. He's more interested in forming us into the image of His Son than He is in moving us out of our situations. He desires to bring all that is in our renewed spirit into our souls, so that our behavior is godly.

The process of godly change should be worth more to us than anything else. It does not matter to God how much it costs in the natural realm to form the image of Christ in us.

Maybe we don't like to lose money, reputation, or friends, but God does not mind if we lose these things to get His Son formed in us. The training may cost a lot to us, but it's nothing to God. He can replace anything it might cost. Whatever the devil means for evil, God can make it for good. That is one of the unique abilities of God.

When we get to know God better, some of these other things that we're seeking will begin to diminish in importance. This is when we start becoming a partner with God in prayer. Instead of always going to God with all the things we want, we begin to see the things that God wants to do in our lives and in the world around us. Then we go to God to ask His will and begin to see things happen.

Let's let the majority of our petitions to God be, "Lord, change me. Lord, let your kingdom come into my life."

For just a few minutes, let's just forget about the houses, boyfriends, cars, husbands, children, health, careers, etc. Let's learn to seek Him first, and He'll add all of these other things to us.

To whom do we direct our petitions?

One last thing about petitions. Our requests should be made to God the Father. Sometimes people make requests to Jesus. It is all right to thank Jesus for what He accomplished on the cross. It is all right to acknowledge the help of the Holy Spirit in teaching us and guiding us, but when it comes to petitions, the Scripture teaches that we should make these to the Father. In the model prayer of Matthew 6:9 in which Jesus instructed the disciples, he tells them to begin by saying, "Our Father who art in heaven. . ."

The Holy Spirit is present with us, and it is all right to carry on a conversation with the Holy Spirit as we go about our day. But when we talk about entering the throne room with our petitions, those should be addressed to our Father in heaven. Elsewhere in the gospels, Jesus tells us to pray to the Father in His name (John 15:16; 16:23). Nowhere are we told to bring our petitions to Jesus or the Holy Spirit.

Summary

When we begin to ask God to change us, we'll see changes in our circumstances and in our world. God can change us to manifest His unconditional love. That love is already within Christians. God brings it out by changing our emotional and thinking patterns. Love increases power in prayer. God's priority is His people.

Questions for thought and action

1. When you face a difficult situation or person, do you normally ask God to: (1) Change the situation or person; (2) Change you and your ability to love; or (3) Remove you from the problem?

2. Which ones of the following are blocking God's love in your life?
jealousy   conceit   rudeness   touchiness   gossip   slander
unforgiveness   selfishness   possessiveness   resentfulness insecurity   self pity   envy

3. In the last difficult situation or person you faced, what was God trying to bring out from your spirit to your soul?   faith   kindness
patience   endurance   other_____

4. If it is true that people who offend us are just asking us for prayer, write down the last two people who put in a prayer request to you.

5. (From Question #4): Did you complete the assignment God's way? What could you have done differently?

Chapter 9

Seek

But seek ye first the kingdom of God and his righteousness; and all these things shall be added unto you. **Matthew 6:33**
Again, the kingdom of heaven is like unto a merchant man, seeking goodly pearls: who, when he had found one pearl of great price, went and sold all that he had, and bought it. **Matthew 13:45,46**

Seeking God with our all means we are willing to give up everything in order to find the pearl of great price. Seeking God indicates a willingness to put everything we cherish, depend upon, and consider important aside and let God become most important in our lives. The prayer which pushes us toward that goal is the *prayer of unconditional surrender* to God. In it we tell God that nothing matters to us more than His Spirit controlling us.

In the prayer of unconditional surrender, we tell God the rule of His kingdom in our lives is more important to us than our careers, families, ministries, reputation, possessions, money, or anything else we value. And we give Him permission to test us on any of these points.

Let God be God

We say we love and worship God, but often we are just in love with the traditions and structures of our religious systems. We don't mind being religious as long as we can do what we want to do. We don't mind going to church as long as we can go wherever we want the other days in the week. We can be religious as long as religion doesn't keep us from doing our own thing.

What we need more than anything else is to let God be God in our lives. He must be in complete control. Kingdom means reign. As we seek God's kingdom, we let God have more and more control over our lives. Our security, worth, hope, expectation, confidence, attention, purpose, and identity must be in God alone. We must turn to Him only for comfort, wisdom, energy, resources, and motivation.

Be warned: it is possible to make this commitment, forget it, and go on about our business, gradually losing the fervor we have for the Lord. The unconditional surrender prayer is not a "one time only" prayer. We will need to remind ourselves often and reaffirm to God that we still are holding on to our initial commitment.

For too long as a race, we have looked to the government, the lottery, our jobs, and everything else to be the provider of our needs. We have looked to many things for comfort. We have looked to guns to be our protection, preachers and evangelists to be our teachers and guides. We have sought to find strength in organizations, church structures, and legislation; worth and acceptance in positions and titles. We need to repent of having all of these other gods before the one and only true God.

Deuteronomy 5:7,9 says: "Thou shalt have none others gods before me. Thou shalt not bow down thyself unto them, nor serve them; for I the Lord thy God am a jealous God, visiting the iniquity of the fathers upon the children unto the third and fourth generation of them that hate me."

Deuteronomy 28:15,20 tells us the consequences of not seeking: "But it shall come to pass, if thou wilt not hearken unto the voice of the Lord thy God,. . . the Lord shall send upon thee cursing, vexation, and rebuke,. in all that thou settest thine hand unto for to do, until thou be destroyed, and until thou perish quickly; because of the wickedness of thy doings, whereby thou hast forsaken me."

God is God. Nothing changes that. We spoke of His resume, but it did not include all that He is. There is no other "god" like Him. There is no other "god" beside Him. Everything else is false. Everything else is a front for the enemy of God.

God is the God of all comfort (2 Corinthians 1:3). He is all powerful. God is our provider. God is wisdom and peace. He desires to function as our one and only God. He wants to determine our priorities in life. In order to let God be God, we will have to be rid of all other false gods.

If we know the false gods in our lives, we can voluntarily surrender them to God. However, many of us are not even aware of how many occupy our hearts. We do not have to worry. God can show us if we ask Him. Even if we don't ask, He has ways of exposing them.

The most important prayer

The unconditional surrender prayer may well be the most important prayer we pray. If we do not pray this prayer, most other praying will be in vain.

The unconditional surrender prayer is essential to finding our way back into the protecting arms of God.

A lot of people treat God like a big granddad in the sky who will give everything they ask. But we need to get past that stage. As we grow, there are more and more responsibilities on our part. One thing we must do as we grow is to give God our all.

At a certain point of growth, God's response to us is based on how much of ourselves we give to Him. Frankly, He is not satisfied with less than everything. This is because He wants to give His everything to us. But if we hold back, He'll hold back. Then we're disappointed in Him and hold back some more. He'll respond likewise. We should be drawing near to God; for as we draw near to God, He will draw near to us (James 4:8).

God wants unconditional surrender. He wants us to seek Him first. He wants us to seek Him with all of our heart, soul, mind, and strength. He promises if we seek Him with our all we will find Him. "Then shall ye call upon me, and ye shall go and pray unto me, and I will hearken unto you. And ye shall seek me, and find me, when ye shall search for me with all your heart. And I will be found of you, saith the Lord: and I will turn away your captivity" (Jeremiah 29:11-13).

The attachments of our hearts

As long as we attach our heart to other things, we are selling ourselves short. We also do not allow God to fully work in our lives. God can do some great and powerful things in our lives, but we limit God by not giving Him everything. That's why the searchlight prayer is so important. It can show us the things to which our hearts are attached.

If we don't pray the prayer of unconditional surrender and allow God to bring it to pass in our lives, our Christian lives will just continue to go in circles. We will never get full victory. We will never get to a place of intimacy with God.

We do not have to wait until we're certain God is number one before we pray this prayer. When we pray this prayer, God can then begin the lifetime process of making Himself number one in our lives.

As God becomes first in our lives, other priorities will be shifted. The process of reducing the importance of other things in our lives is not pleasant, but is necessary in order for God to take His rightful place as God. This is the process of knowing God.

The pain causes many people to either stand still or turn back. There is legitimate pain as God takes us from the realm of body/souls to become spirit/souls, training us to walk in the Spirit. They are growing pains.

The walk in the Spirit is nothing at all like the natural walk. In order for us to learn it, we are often taken through circumstances designed to force us to stay dependent upon God. These circumstances can cause temporary pain to our flesh.

Because of a waiting time between the promise of God and its fulfillment, we often become impatient and run away from God into enemy territory. When we are deceived into thinking pain is to be avoided at all cost, we often refuse to grow up and thus continue as prey for the enemy.

Being open with God
Part of unconditional surrender is being open with God. It's okay to tell Him where you really are. It's even okay to tell God we're not sure if it is really safe to give Him unconditional surrender. We'll call this prayer the *prayer of transparency.*

When we hurt, feel depressed, or doubtful, we can tell God about it. God can handle our honesty.

Someone once told me of a time when she was experiencing lots of problems on her job. It was very frustrating for her. She really wanted God to be first in her life, but could not understand why He allowed all of the things that were happening. I smiled when she told me what she said to God. It truly was a prayer of transparency. She told God, "Lord, my name is not Job"!

She was serious. She was fed up with the many problems. Guess what. God did not strike her dead. In fact, she grew in intimacy with Him. He comforted her. When she was telling me about it all, she was praising God for His miraculous deliverance out of her troubles. She knew God had done it. She also understood how the enemy had used the people on her job to get at her. She did not stay mad at God when she recognized her *real enemy.* I don't think she would have had the victory and the insight if she had held in her frustration with God and *pretended* she was pleased with how He was handling things.

Some Christians can't admit they are depressed. Many times we pretend we are at peace when we are not. Sometimes we are angry with God, and will not admit it because we feel we have to keep up a front. If we are angry, worried, or depressed; we should admit it to God and allow Him to minister to us.

We cannot expect God to change our emotions if we refuse to acknowledge them. Sometimes we are so separated (broken) we do not even realize what is going on in our emotions.

Praising God in everything does not mean we live in denial. We can admit how we feel and still ask God to give us strength to praise Him even though we do not feel like it. It may be a sacrifice. We then ask Him to help our emotions follow along.

Practical application of the prayer of transparency

Let's look at how this might work on a practical level in relationships. Let's say somebody in the church has made you angry. You may need to go to God and have a heart-to-heart talk. Let Him know the person did really hurt you. You might say, "I'm angry about what Sister So-and-So did. It hurt. But I know that you are the God of all comfort. I need a touch of your comfort to relieve my pain." You don't have to pretend you did not get hurt.

After our little talk with God, God may indicate He wants to help Sister So-and-So. He might tell you to go to her and let her know that it hurt you. You're not trying to hurt her or to tell her off. It's purely out of a motive of love. Perhaps this is a pattern that has alienated her from others in the past.

Getting to know God

One of the really good ways to get to know God is to meditate upon Him and remind ourselves of who He is in spite of our circumstances. If our circumstances are undesirable, the enemy will have us believing God does not love us, or He is not powerful. Even if it seems that God is not doing anything, we should still praise Him for who He is and what He is. He is still God, regardless of our circumstances.

Most Christians really don't know God. We know a lot about Him, and that's good. It's good to know about Him. But we should really get to know His character. The mere fact we do not praise Him more is an indication we do not know Him well. The more you know God, the more you'll fall in love with Him, and the more you will cease to worry about the trials and difficulties you encounter.

When we do that over and over, we expand our worship in prayer. After continuing in this way for some time God will reveal His character. This is how we learn to know God.

When we talk about praying, we are talking about coming into the presence of God Almighty, the Creator, the One who upholds the whole universe by the Word of His power. We are talking about the One and only true God. We're speaking of One who owns and made all things.

Isaiah 40:12 gives us some insight as to who God is: "Who hath measured the waters in the hollow of his hand, and meted out heaven with the span, and comprehended the dust of the earth in a measure, and weighed the mountains in scales, and the hills in a balance?"

Remember God's resume? He's in control of everything. Nothing happens without His knowledge. He has all power, knows everything and is everywhere. When we go to God in prayer, we're going into the throne room of God to have an audience with the One who holds this world in His hand. When you really meditate on that, it is awesome.

Most of us will never have the privilege of getting a personal audience with the President of the United States. But what if we did? Would we run in, blurt out a few requests, and run back out?

"Definitely not," you say. But isn't that just what we sometimes do when we're in the presence of God Almighty? We don't always fully comprehend the awesome nature of that privilege, do we?

Praise is part of seeking

You know what? A lot of people would have us believe their Bibles read, "come into His presence with crying, whining, and complaining."

The first words we need to utter when we come to God are words of thanksgiving and praise. In doing this, we acknowledge the greatness of the One to whom we are talking. Let us look again to the Scriptures for insight into these *prayers of worship*.

Psalm 100:1-2 says, "Make a joyful noise unto the Lord, all ye lands. Serve the Lord with gladness: come before His presence with singing." What is a joyful noise? It could be whatever you are comfortable with. Some people might be comfortable with shouting, "Hallelujah." Others may be more comfortable with singing a song of praise. Either one is a joyful noise.

Verse 3 says, "Know ye that the Lord he is God: it is he that hath made us, and not we ourselves; we are his people, and the sheep of his pasture." In this verse, we are reminded of whom we are addressing. When we do not realize the Lord is God, sometimes we treat Him as our servant. We did not make ourselves, He made us. We are His sheep, His people. He owns us, we do not own Him. It is important that we remind ourselves of this. Otherwise, we come to Him with attitudes of pride and arrogance.

Now we can enter His gates with thanksgiving and His courts with praise as indicated in verse 4. It is with an attitude of thankfulness that we are to bring our petitions and supplications to God.

Verse 4 tells us to "be thankful unto him, and bless his name." The word *bless* comes from a root word that means to kneel. It has the idea of salute and praise. So when we bless His name, we acknowledge that we are beneath Him in status. He is One to whom we bow. We come with an attitude of reverence. We offer praise and adoration to Him.

It is also appropriate to physically kneel when we come to talk to Him. Kneeling is a recommended posture. Again this helps the natural attitude of pride that is very much part of our flesh. Other postures are also Scriptural.

In verse 5, we are again reminded of the character of God. This verse tells us "the Lord is good, his mercy is everlasting; and his truth endureth to all generations." The Lord is good. His goodness may be blocked and our experience may not be in agreement with this fact. However, let us not create additional blocks. Let us agree with God's Word that He is good. With time our circumstances will come in line with truth.

Thanksgiving and praise are really more for us than for God. Our God is great, mighty, merciful, and kind; and it is more than appropriate to praise and thank Him for being who He is. We acknowledge truth with our lips even if our emotions do not feel up to it. We enter into His gates with thanksgiving and into His courts with praise. This can be done in song, spoken words, or both.

We can thank God not only for who He is, but for what He has already done. For starters, we can thank God that Jesus paved the way for us to come into His presence. We can thank Him for mercy and grace that allows us as humans to benefit from His goodness. We can thank Him for the cleansing of sin and righteousness provided through His Son. There are so many things for which to be thankful and to give Him praise.

Scriptural examples

The Scriptures give us some examples of prayers of worship. Here's one, "And the Levites, of the children of the Kohathites, and of the children of the Korhites, stood up to praise the Lord God of Israel with a loud voice on high" (2 Chronicles 20:19).

Did those Levites get a little carried away or what? Standing up and getting loud. My word. But they did not stop there. The next day when they were ready to go into battle, they appointed singers unto the Lord whose sole job was to sing and to praise the Lord.

Even the King Jehoshaphat seemed to go a little overboard by putting his face to the ground in worshipping the Lord according to 2 Chronicles 20:18. Does it really take all of that?

You can never praise God enough. God's strong presence is in the praise of His people (Psalms 22:3).

There is room for individuality in praise styles. A naturally quiet person may want to make a joyful noise by singing a song of thanksgiving. Another person may want to shout, sing and then thank God for fifteen minutes before he brings his petitions. Others might want to lift their hands, clap, or dance. All Scriptural methods are valid.

Summary

Seeking God with our all involves an attitude of giving up everything in the prayer of unconditional surrender. We realize that the pearl of great price—having God control our lives—is worth our entire life. As we must humbly ask God to teach us to walk in the Spirit, we willingly surrender ideas of what it means to be a successful Christian and accept the possibility of learning all over again. As we get to know God, we open up our feelings to Him in prayers of transparency.

The ultimate goal is to love God with all our heart, soul, mind and strength, and to love our neighbor as ourselves. Just as we cannot seek God only in part, we can't love God with a little bit; we have to give our all. That means that we have to take all the things that we are seeking or love and bring them under the love to God. God can help us to distribute our love everywhere else as long as He has it all.

But if we try to divide our love ourselves or love with conditions ("Lord, I'll love you if you will only do this"), it won't work. If we are honest with ourselves, we will see that we love a lot of things more than God.

We go to God to make requests with the proper attitude—attitudes of thanksgiving, praise, adoration in prayers of worship. We come to Him with singing, joyfulness, and gladness. We come to Him in humility, bowing before Him.

Cultivating a lifestyle of praise and thanksgiving is essential to one who desires to be used of God in prayer. And yes, it might even be necessary to get loud at times when we praise God. We may even get a little emotional and shed a few tears when we think of the goodness of God. For some, these methods of praise may not be customary. But change is in order if we want to turn our hearts toward God.

Questions for thought and action

1. Either in the past or the present, name some of the things that bring you security or worth. To help, fill in the blanks: I don't believe I could ever do without_____, or I don't know what I would do if _____ were taken away from me. (friends, spouse, children, job, career, house, car, health, reputation, ministry, possessions, parents, habits, etc.).

2. Have you ever prayed the "prayer of unconditional surrender" at any time in your life? And did you ever realize you needed to remind yourself of it?   ____YES ____NO ; ____YES ____NO

3. If you had to estimate what "percentage" of yourself was given over to seeking God, what would it be? ____25% or less ____25-50% ____50-75% ____75-90% ____90-95%

4. How often do you express your honest negative emotions to God, such as fear, doubt, anger, lust, hate,etc. ____NEVER ____OCCA-SIONALLY ____SOMETIMES ____FREQUENTLY

5. Do you always need a church setting to worship God or have you learned to worship God in the privacy of your home? ____I need a church setting ____I worship God in my home ____I find myself worshipping God in my car, at home, anywhere.

Chapter 10

Turn

That in reference to your former manner of life, you lay aside the old self, which is being corrupted in accordance with the lusts of deceit, and that you be renewed in the spirit of your mind, and put on the new self, which in the likeness of God has been created in righteousness and holiness of the truth. **Ephesians 4:22-24,** NAS

The last ingredient in our four-part recipe is to turn from our wicked ways. This is the action. It is most appropriate to talk about turning as we approach the end of our prayer journey. If you start at the very beginning of the prayer recipe, and put in the first three ingredients, turning is the logical conclusion. It is the action of putting off the old ways and putting on the ways of God.

Know ye not, that so many of us as were baptized into Jesus Christ were baptized into his death? Therefore we are buried with him by baptism into death: that like as Christ was raised up from the dead by the glory of the Father, even so we also should walk in newness of life. For if we have been planted together in the likeness of his death, we shall be also in the likeness of his resurrection: Knowing this, that our old man is crucified with him, that the body of sin might

be destroyed, that henceforth we should not serve sin. For he that is
dead is freed from sin. Romans 6:3-7

The above Scripture passage tells us our old nature died with
Christ. It's not a sinful nature we have within us which we're strug-
gling against, it's the flesh. Sometimes as an excuse we'll say, "Well,
you know, I still have my old sinful nature. I can't do any better."
Wrong. We've got the nature of God in us. The old nature has been
crucified at the cross.

But we still have memories of old thought and emotional patterns.
That's the flesh, the old self according to the opening Scripture in
this chapter. That's what we are to put off. We are not to walk in the
way of the old man or flesh. We are to walk in the way of the Spirit.
We *can* choose to do better.

There is a big difference. Instead of an old nature we can't do
anything about, we have attitudes, emotions, and thinking patterns
we can put off. When we choose the old instead of the new way
deposited within our spirits, we continue to live fleshly lives. If we
walk in the Spirit, we do not fulfill the lust of the flesh (Galatians 5:16).

The war is a dual one. We are fighting both against our flesh
(Galatians 5:16-21), and against evil spirits (Ephesians 6:12). Sometimes, we must fight both at the same time. The flesh gives the hooks
into our lives the enemy needs. Walking in the Spirit eliminates those
hooks.

Satan's cohorts were instrumental in creating the hooks by ar-
ranging situations as early as childhood which left certain emotional
and thought programs. These programs are the old patterns of hate,
anger, or insecurity which rise to the surface under the "right"
circumstances.

Choosing the new instead of the old

The act of turning is the entrance into victorious living. It begins when we change our ways of thinking and responding. By responding in the flesh, we block the Holy Spirit from changing our soul.

Most Christians are taught to live the Christian life by the strength of their soul; that is, their mind, will and emotion. However, *the soul is a part of the flesh if it does not draw its strength from the Spirit.*

The way of the Spirit produces the fruit of the Spirit: love, joy, peace, patience, gentleness, goodness, meekness, temperance, and faith. God the Holy Spirit can begin a work of turning in our attitudes, behavior, and reactions. But it is up to us to accept and use what has been provided. We simply must look to the Word of God and make the decision to change.

The struggle is one of choices. As we increase choosing the way of the Spirit, we strengthen new circuits in our minds which feed back into our behavior. The movement is upward; we are continually becoming more like Jesus.

Of course, we can refuse to turn and experience more of the enemy's bondages and schemes in our lives and the lives of those in our families. It's our choice. I know Christians who have had difficulty turning. Their decision to keep an old way eventually led to a lost of many things—family, children, jobs, cars, peace, joy, ministry, and reputation. Thank God, many have decided their old ways are not worth keeping. Thank God, He still loves and accepts each person and will give them strength to turn to ways that will bless their lives.

The wicked way of wrong motivations

Some of our wicked ways seem right in our own eyes, but they are not the ways of God. He desires to remove even our "good" out of us if it is there by our own strength, on the shaky foundation of wrong motivations.

You might be praying or ministering publicly to impress others. You might be witnessing primarily to gain God's approval and acceptance. You might be trying to get your children to live right because you're embarrassed by their ungodly behavior. These are serious offenses to the cross of Christ.

Most of the time, we do not even consciously know we are operating from wrong or mixed motivations. We do not know our own hearts. God looks at the heart and not the outward behavior.

The light of God can expose the wrong motives. Paul, in Ephesians 5:11-14, speaks of the light reproving (exposing) the unfruitful works of darkness. If we are faithful to the searchlight prayer to ask God to show us our hearts, the prayer of confession to admit what He shows us, then we have to be faithful to turn from the old ways.

Prejudice: one of the worst offenses

What are the wicked ways of the people of God? One of them is the tendency to judge others by outward appearance. It happened even in the early church. Much of the book of first Corinthians deals with immaturity because of divisions and prejudice (1:10-12, 3:1-5, 11:17-22, 12:12-27,13:4-7).

Paul in 1 Corinthians 11:29 and 30 says that weakness, sickness and premature death occurred among the people of God because they did not "discern the Lord's body." Taking the Lord's supper unworthily has something to do with improperly respecting or recognizing all members of God's family. Today it could very well mean women, black, or poor members.

The folks whom God addresses in the book of James seemed to have a problem in this area as well (James 2:1-12). They were giving special time and attention to those who had money and ignoring the poor. They were the living embodiment of the verse in 1 Samuel 16:7, ". . . man looks at the outward appearance." But, to continue that verse, ". . . the Lord looks at the heart."

James tells us, "But if ye have respect to person, ye commit sin, and are convicted of the law as transgressors." If we are going to be children of God, we must learn to judge as He judges . . . after the heart.

Isaiah 11:3 says that God will make Jesus "of quick understanding in the fear of the Lord," and that Jesus "shall not judge after the sight of his eyes, neither reprove after the hearing of his ears." Jesus' ways are righteous.

When we judge someone or something by external characteristics, that is wicked. This includes judging someone by their size, their color, their gender, doctrinal beliefs, education, social status, or any other criteria. We all have been guilty.

Judgmental and critical attitudes without a commitment to laying our lives down in prayer and a willingness to be used of God to come along beside another for restoration is a wicked way. We may be accurate in our assessment of how bad a person is; but God did not call us to assessment. He called us to be agents of change.

Instead of condemning based on appearance, we should ask the Lord to help us understand the person. Perhaps we'll find a broken heart there. If we are in a spiritual position to restore the person, that should be our next step (Galatians 6:1).

God called us to destroy the works of the enemy. He called us to heal the broken-hearted and give sight to the blind. As much as we might kid ourselves, we will not be able to effectively carry out our mission of being change agents as long as we allow attitudes of criticism and discrimination to remain in our hearts. Let us ask God to expose the places in our lives in which we are quick to judge. Let us turn from those ways.

How should we talk to God?
Often we come to God with this tone and attitude: "God! I don't know how long it's going to take you to do this simple thing. You really don't

have too good a track record with me . . . ." We're not actually saying this to Him—we may say something like, "Lord, you know I need a car," or "How long do I have to wait for a husband, Lord?"— but it is in our emotions and comes out in our attitude. We must turn from coming to God in this manner. The discussion on praise in the last chapter gives us the appropriate way to enter into God's presence.

Summary
The writer of Hebrews in chapter 4:6 speaks of a rest for the people of God that we must labor to enter. As we learn to depend upon God, we will eventually abide in Him, instead of running back and forth.

Defeat will be certain if we think we must be ruled by a sinful nature. Nothing can be done about a nature. But there is hope when we realize that the nature of God is within us, and He will help us renew our minds. Romans 12:2 says, "Be transformed by the renewing of your minds, that you may prove what the will of God is, that which is good and acceptable and perfect."

The process of turning is painful. It means letting go of habits and attitudes with which you have grown accustomed. But what you gain is far more valuable. It is even more painful to refuse to turn. The next chapter will show us how to cope with the pain as it describes the process by which the prayer ingredients are "cooked in the oven."

Questions for thought and action

1. Have you ever prayed for someone's salvation in which your motives were mixed? _____YES _____NO

2. Have you ever been convicted that you shared a victory in ministering, witnessing or prayer because you wanted to make a good impression? _____YES _____NO

3. Complete the following: My Christianity is characterized by: _____ struggle _____rest _____combination of both.

4. What kind of people do you have trouble treating without prejudice?_____handicapped _____ foreign born
_____wealthy people _____another political party
_____ men _____other races
_____another denomination _____Other_____

5.How much turning do you have to do in coming to God in prayer?
_____I come to God with Thanksgiving and praise most of the time.
_____I come with Thanksgiving and praise about half. _____I come with complaints most of the time.

Chapter 11

Baptism of fire

John answered, saying unto them all, I indeed baptize you with water; but one mightier than I cometh, the latchet of whose shoes I am not worthy to unloose: he shall baptize you with the Holy Ghost and with fire: Whose fan is in his hand, and he will thoroughly purge his floor, and will gather the wheat into his garner; but the chaff he will burn with fire unquenchable. **Luke 3:16,17**

It was a dream, but it was very real. She was driving her car on a windy country road when everything suddenly went pitch black. There were no lights, not even in the car. Knowing that the road was full of curves, the driver decided to pull over and wait. But at that moment Jesus appeared and said, "Let me take over. I'll drive from here."

The warning
We have gone through each ingredient of the prayer recipe. We have looked at instructions on how to mix it all together. Now all we have to do is put it in the oven. The oven is a baptism of fire.

The baptism of fire is not comfortable. It is a place of intense heat. It is designed to burn off anything that may hinder your growth in the kingdom. It's a time of great darkness, a time when you want to pull over and not continue on the journey.

God shakes those things out of us so that only what cannot be shaken is left. The fire of God then consumes the shaken things so we might receive His kingdom (Hebrews 12:26-29). Maybe your life is going through a "shake and bake" process. Rejoice, it might be from God. This chapter will help you come out intact without smelling like smoke.

The fire this time . . .

The enemy is content as long as you walk in darkness. As you move through the prayer recipe and toward the light, he is going to be disturbed. He will be downright angry as he knows he is about to lose one of the greatest assets to his work: a Christian whose light does not shine.

He will increase his attacks against us. If in the past, we were assigned three demons, he might well increase it to thirty demons. These demons will operate in the people and circumstances around us. Things will get so weird at times we will contemplate giving up and returning to the mundane life of a "good American Christian."

The pressures will be great. The enemy will try to touch the most vulnerable areas of your life. For some, it will be money or possessions. For others, it might be health.

. . . hits us on the inside, too

As your outside circumstances change, it is possible your mind, will, and emotions—your flesh—will go haywire. Your mind will tell you it is not worth all the pain. Discouragement, depression, or rage might be in your emotions as you try to cope in your own strength. You will find things coming out you never knew were in you.

That is the enemy's objective. He will try to take away your peace, joy, and unconditional love for God. As a result, you will be tempted to turn back. The stress may be that great.

Often the enemy will try to hit you in just the place where God wants to give you a ministry. If finances are a great struggle, it is possible God has a ministry of giving for you in His kingdom. If brokenness has been your plight, God may desire to use you to bring wholeness to others.

The flesh does not want God to be in control. We find it more comfortable to walk after our own understanding than to acknowledge Him in all our ways, letting him direct our paths. Life in the Spirit means self has to die. It's much easier to live a religious life than to live a life of the Spirit in total dependency upon God.

We do not learn to live until we die (2 Corinthians 4:10-12).

The baptism of fire is a cleansing process. Our pride will be touched. We will have to face up to a lot of dirty laundry. It may be very embarrassing as others see it. Buried junk in our lives will be brought to the surface so it can be skimmed off.

I always thought I was pretty good at forgiving others until the Lord allowed some experiences that brought a lot of hate and bitterness to the surface. Actually, it wasn't that I was that good at forgiving, but because of Christian training, I had learned to suppress my anger. The Lord was determined to get at the roots of anger, but as long as I would not face it, He couldn't do anything with it. The traumatic experiences were necessary in order for God to confront and change me.

Only then was I ready for re-programming. The experiences were very painful. We experience major surgery in the spiritual realm as God changes us. Surgery is painful.

But God is in the midst of the fire. He knows the very idols that we trust and is giving us the chance to let them go so that we might and love and serve Him with our all. He is answering the prayers of the prayer recipe. We have asked Him to search us and cleanse us. We have surrendered all of our life to Him and have said that we make Him first and want nothing else to take His rightful place as Lord.

We do not know our own hearts. "The heart is deceitful above all things, and desperately wicked: who can know it? I the Lord search the heart, I try the reins [emotions], even to give every man according to his ways, and according to the fruit of his doings" (Jeremiah 17:9,10).

We do not know our own hearts. God shows us our hearts and gives us a chance to turn from our wicked ways. He gives us a chance to anchor our souls completely in Him. As we let go of all of the other things that we are attached to, we will be free to be anchored in Him.

But it is for a reason

God is working in us a dependency upon Himself. Dependency upon God is precious. That's what God desperately wants to develop in us. As in the dream, we will drive as long as we see our way. God lets it get dark so we are forced to stop. Then we are more willing to let Him take over.

The goal of the adversary is to get us out from under the covering of God's favor. His purpose is to keep us at a distance from God and get us to think that God Himself is actually the cause of the painful experiences we go through. If we are closer to the enemy than we are to God, we will actually blame God for our problems. When we do, we can actually fall into the enemy's snare.

Imagine this conversation: "Why do I have to go through all this pain? The *other person* ran over my leg. I didn't have a choice. Why do I have to be the one to get my leg set. This is too painful. Doctor, you must hate me!"

It is very easy to forget God's love for us when we are in pain. God loves us so much He gave the life of His only Son to make a way for us to live with Him and enjoy His goodness. Unfortunately, sometimes our former way of living keeps His goodness from us. Learning to live in His ways has the ultimate goal of good, but there is pain first.

The pain is God's way of keeping us close to Himself. It can serve many purposes. It can move us to come back underneath His protective wings. It can teach us about the goodness of God. It can spur us to spiritual growth.

God brings adverse circumstances and difficult people into our lives. The adverse circumstances purify our love for God. The difficult people help to purify our love for others. "Knowing this, that the trying of your faith worketh patience. But let patience have her perfect work, that ye may be perfect and entire, wanting nothing" (James 1:3,4).

These people and situations show us what is in our hearts. We may be able to put on a pretty good front most of the time, but we can't hide when God allows our lives to be stirred up.

God has the same faith in us as He did in Job, that we will not curse Him or love Him any less. He's waiting for the time He can restore back to us twice what was taken. But Satan is trying as hard as he can to get us to believe his lie that God does not love us and does not have our best interests at heart.

In the meantime, God is actually using the trials and tribulations to burn the flesh. God does not waste anything. Even what the enemy intends for evil, God can recycle for His glory.

Because of our broken hearts, a hard shell of protection surrounds our lives. Vessels God has chosen have to be broken again, this time by God, so His Spirit can be released.

The fire actually serves as training for God's army. Those who are aware they are in boot camp should not give up. Press on through to the glory, the presence of God. Trade in the pain for the glory.

For many, the fire is here

Fortunately, many African American women do not have the fiery furnace to look forward to. They are in it now. Many of us have been undergoing boot camp for years and have not even understood what was going on. Rejection, financial difficulties, waiting for God's promises—these are all part of the fire.

Part of the reason it has lasted so long is because we have not cooperated with God. We have actually been angry with God. The boot camp experience is designed to come to an end. We will then be equipped to help others undergo this necessary cleansing.

Everybody will have to undergo a baptism of fire. There is really no option if we are going to be the people God wants. African American women who have lived in the fire can serve as guides to those who still have it ahead of them.

What to do when "going through"

It is encouraging to see what God is doing in the lives of many women. However, it is discouraging to realize that some, in not understanding what God is doing, have become confused and angry, and have even resisted God's work. Proper understanding is vital.

Some of us have more stubbornness and pride to be burned off than others. We cannot necessarily shorten the time required for God to complete His work, but we could prolong it. Admitting we have complained, murmured, or been full of unbelief is the first step in coming out of a rut. Continuing all of the prayer steps—humility, commitment, seeking, turning—should keep us moving through.

It cannot be repeated too often that God really does love us. *Jesus loves you. You are fully accepted in Christ.* As difficult as it may be to believe when we are in the "fire", we have to stand on that truth. It is the rock that will help us keep our sanity. It is often helpful to remind ourselves of the truth of God's love daily. We can also offer a sacrifice of praise to God for His love—in spite of our circumstances (Hebrews 13:15,16). These practices will help us to go on through the fire. We don't want to stay in it. The fire is not meant to last forever.

The quickest way to get out of the fire is to learn to pray for and bless those—be they friend, foe, or family—who are causing us the pain in our furnace of fire. We can move into the realm of the Spirit by praying for the persons Satan has used against us. For African American women, this may mean whites and men who may have been a destructive influence.

Again, just as a reminder, our prayer for them is not for them to get out of our lives. Our prayer is for them to experience God's forgiveness, love, blessing, goodness, and healing.

It is very likely that Saul of Tarsus in Acts 9 had such a dramatic conversion experience because of the kinds of prayers mentioned above were prayed for him. When the new Christians began to murmur and complain about being persecuted, the Apostles probably reminded them of the teachings of the Lord Jesus Christ that they should pray for their enemies. With that much prayer, the poor guy didn't have a chance. Our prayers will not only change us, but can also open the door for God to deal with the person.

We must also pray the prayers previously discussed—confession, transparency, and asking. The prayer of confession allows us to appropriate the provision of the cross and the blood of Jesus. We simply remind ourselves and agree with God that the blood of Jesus covers all of our sins and failures. Instead of providing our own inadequate covering, we allow Him to cover us. The prayer of transparency allows us to be honest about our weakness, without blaming, denying, rationalizing, or excusing ourselves. We ask God to change us. We also continue to cast our cares on Him and renew our unconditional surrender as many times as needed.

The prayers of the prayer recipe are our keys to getting through this dark period. They force us to depend upon God.

Another prayer

As we progress on this journey into the reality of God's kingdom ruling in our lives and experience trials and difficulties, we are tempted to try to make it on our own. God will let us exhaust all of our own means until we are in a corner with nowhere to go.

When we ask Him to remove the source of pain. He tells us, "My grace is sufficient for you; my strength is made perfect in weakness" (2 Corinthians 12:9).

Finally, we get the point and begin to call out to God with another prayer. This prayer was not discussed in the prayer recipe. But in a way, it is a combination of all of the prayers introduced. It is the prayer for grace. It is a simple request for help. Let's call it the *SOS prayer.*

When you send a SOS, the shorter the better. "Help" or Help, Lord" is simple enough. Sometimes that is all we can get out.

Our spiritual maturing will bring us into more of a dependency upon God. We'll find ourselves praying "SOS"-like prayers more, not less. The tricks and deceptions of the enemy will be so intensified that we'll need God more than ever.

How many times did we miss the opportunity that God was using to force us to lean upon Him and not to our own understanding?

No time for pain

After the prayers, we submit ourselves to the fire, the trial of our faith. Let us submit ourselves under the mighty hand of God. God knows the wicked ways in each of us. The fire will burn it all, unless we resist or stay angry with God.

Sometimes as we go through the fire, we experience an intensified feeling of grief over all the pain buried in our hearts, pain we may have pushed down as a means of survival. Often we may find ourselves crying for no apparent reason. At this point, it is vital we go to God for comfort as we let the tears flow.

If our pain has never experienced God's comfort, perhaps we have been turning to other temporary places for comfort. We are not promising getting rid of pain overnight, but there is relief. No matter how great the pain, we can get comfort from God. He is the God of all comfort (2 Corinthians 1:3).

Finally, let us rejoice in the wonderful work God is doing in our life. "Count it all joy when ye fall into divers temptations" (James 1:2).

After the fire

The fiery phase is temporary. It will not last forever. Our growth in grace and in the knowledge of God will continue as long as we live, but this major cleansing will not last beyond what is necessary. Even in the future, as God continues to expose areas needing cleansing, it will not be as painful as this initial time.

Also after the fire, we'll go out to rescue others because we have learned to operate under the full protection of God. After our fiery furnace, we will receive the enabling from God to defeat the devil in others' lives. In the meantime, many others are still in need of comfort. In our own pain, God was our comfort, we comfort others with the comfort we received from God (2 Corinthians 1:4).

Many who have been in the fires for years will find that as a result of submitting to the fires, they will be let out of the furnace. The end result will be similar to the three Hebrew boys in the book of Daniel. Not only were the ropes of bondage burned, but the boys were also joined by one who was like the Son of God (Daniel 3:25).

This is the hope to which we look forward. After our ropes are burned and the Spirit is released through the brokenness of the outer man, we also will experience sweet fellowship with Jesus Christ. Ironically, in spite of the experience of pain, we will begin to get a fresh understanding of God's love for us as He has finally removed all of the barriers to His goodness.

Many things come as a result of the fire. Yes, disappointments from our sons and daughters, the losses, rejection and pain from our spouses, harassment from our bosses at work, even pain in our bodies are all very unpleasant. But if we only knew what we would receive as a result of it, we'd endure it singing praises to God. Purified precious gold comes out of the fire (1 Peter 1:9).

We will also learn the true meaning of praying "in Jesus' name." Praying in the name of Jesus is more than just tacking a phrase to the end of our prayers. It is praying with the righteousness and lifestyle of Jesus. It comes when God works His life out in our lives. It comes from passing through crises, experiences, and rough terrain. To pray in His name is to live as He lived.

God's presence

The greatest gift at the end of our journey is to have the presence of God on our lives in tangible ways. The suffering will not compare to the glory that shall be. We won't have to wait until heaven to get a taste of the glory, God's presence in our life (Romans 8:17). That's the purpose for which God created us. Through the suffering, we can enter the glory of God.

It is in His presence that we are His friends. It is there we have an open heaven, having the confidence to approach Him.

If we allow patience to have her perfect work in us, we will come out on the other side of this fire. It is with much tribulation that we enter the kingdom (Acts 14:22). After the fiery tribulation, we enter God's reign, the rule of the Spirit. The kingdom brings righteousness, peace and joy (Romans 14:17).

The control of God's Holy Spirit brings the shedding abroad of the love of God in our hearts (Romans 5:2). When we experience and understand God's love for us, we will be free to love our Father with all of our hearts. We will be free to love our neighbors as ourselves.

People who are filled with the Spirit and Word are characterized by singing and making melody in their hearts, singing to each other with songs and psalms and spiritual songs. Two verses that give us the proof of a Spirit-filled life are Colossians 3:16 and Ephesians 5:19. The true evidence of this Spirit/Word-filled life is singing when things are not going right, not when everything is going well (Acts 16). This is a way to know where you are in the process.

Summary

The purpose of spiritual maturity is to love beyond our human capacity. In this way, the Lord exchanges our strength for His strength. If we don't respond God's way, we prolong the trials and increase their severity.

Just knowing a recipe does not produce a dish. We have seen what happens when we put the dish in the oven, the fiery furnace. We have looked at why the fire is so difficult and explored how to make it through.

There are many benefits to "going through"—bondages broken, God's kingdom rule in our life, evidence of the fruit of the Spirit, a new ability to help others, power in prayer, and the glory of God on our lives. Let's be encouraged to press on to the mark of the prize of the high calling of God in Christ Jesus.

As we conclude this section, we have discussed the prayers necessary to change us as individuals. The next section will concentrate on how we now can be keys to change in our homes and communities as we enter another level of prayer—intercession. As we change in our attitudes and behavior, we can help others change.

Questions for thought and action

1. Have you come to the point of having to pray the SOS prayer more? _____YES _____NO

2. Have you been in the fire? _____YES _____NO Have you come through the fire? _____YES _____NO Are you still in the fire? _____YES _____NO or Is the fire yet to come? _____YES _____NO

3. What is your normal tendency towards trials and difficulties? _____complaining _____murmuring _____I try to get others to pity me. _____I'm learning to rejoice. _____I'm not at the rejoicing stage, but I'm learning to be quiet and pray more.

4. Which of the benefits of coming through the fire is most appealing to you? _____presence of God in my life _____weapons to defeat the enemy _____hindrances to walking in the Spirit burned away _____power in prayer

5. Has the fire been prolonged in your life? If so, what do you think is the reason? (Circle as many as appropriate.)
stubbornness   pride   fear   lack of trust in God   anger at God
bitterness towards someone   anger about a circumstance
trying to get through on my own good efforts

Section three: Praying for others

Chapter 12

Heritage of blessings

And it shall come to pass, if thou shalt hearken diligently unto the voice of the Lord thy God, to observe and to do all his commandments which I command thee this day, that the Lord thy God will set thee on high above all nations of the earth: And all these blessings shall come on thee, and overtake thee, if thou shalt hearken unto the voice of the Lord thy God. **Deuteronomy 28:1,2**

God indeed provides a wall of protection for those who walk in obedience to Him. God delights in blessing us. But spiritual laws are in operation. God's whole purpose in giving us the Bible is to show us how to live on the positive side of His spiritual laws.

Satan's whole plan is to trap us into operating on the negative side of the spiritual laws and thereby have God's favor removed. Satan's whole purpose in our life and community is to get us away from the blessings of God. Without the favor of God, we are open targets for the deceiver and all kinds of evil. That's the curse on our communities.

What is a curse? One definition of a curse is "the favor of God turned away from us." God does not delight in our suffering under a curse.

Blocking God's blessings

All of Satan's evil is designed to get us away from the protecting hand of God and to get us to believe God does not have our best interests at heart. The things Satan does are designed to block the blessings of God. We can receive the blessings, however, if we learn the rules. The way has been paved for us to live above the imaginations of the evil one.

God desperately desires to get His goodness and blessing to us. He desires to answer our prayers. It's not a matter of twisting God's arm to get Him to hear our prayers and give us His blessing. The issue is one of removing the blocks that keep the blessings from getting to us. The issue is one of learning how not to participate in activities that already have the curse of God on them. We must learn the ways of the Spirit.

Blessing or Curse: You Can Choose, by Derek Prince states the following:

> The operation of blessings and curses in our lives is not haphazard or unpredictable. On the contrary, both of them operate according to eternal, unchanging laws. It is to the Bible, once again, that we must look for a correct understanding of these laws.
>
> In Proverbs 26:2, Solomon establishes this principle with respect to curses: "A curse without cause shall not alight." Behind every curse that comes upon us, there is a cause. If it seems that we are under a curse, we should seek to determine its cause.

A whole section of the above book is given to studying the Biblical grounds for curses. From Scripture it is pointed out how disrespect for parents, improper use of or disrespect for authority, oppressions against the weak including unborn babies, and the abuse and perversion of the sexual relationship will bring about God's curse.

The enemy has been very clever. As shown in the chapter on "bitter roots," he has put together a well-designed plan to keep the

African American community away from the blessings of God and recipients of the curse of sin. He has lied to us about God. He has arranged and worked through people to substantiate the lies that God is not good, does not have our best interest at heart, and does not hear or answer prayer.

Satan has invested vast amounts of time and energy to keep God's blessing away from African American women. He's done it all, then turns around and accuses God to us. In turn, we live with a hidden rift with God in our emotions. This rift continues to block God's best from getting to us. It also blocks our prayers from getting to God.

We have looked at how African American women have been targets and tools for the enemy. According to 2 Corinthians 2:11, "We are not ignorant of Satan's devices." God has given us understanding in His Word of all that we need to know about the traps of the enemy.

By recognizing the lies of the enemy, women of color can choose to discard them. Few have escaped the enemy's traps. But no matter how successful the enemy has been, where sin abounds, grace abounds all the more (Romans 5:20). God is able to do exceedingly, abundantly more than we can ask or think according to His power that works in us (Galatians 3:20).

God is able to reverse the curse in our families and communities. Through Jesus Christ, we can stop the sins of our natural and spiritual forefathers from passing on any further.

If we continue to follow the prayer recipe, the garbage in our lives will be removed. But we should not be satisfied with just our own freedom. It is extremely important to walk with God to destroy the works of the devil in the lives of our family, friends, and fellow members in the family of God. It is imperative that we live in such a way that we leave blessings for our descendants.

As we begin to walk in truth, we can begin to come out from under the curse of the enemy. We do not have to continue following his every command and reacting the way he has programmed us.

We can learn to really love God with our all. In obeying all His commands, we can be keys to the healing of our community. We can build a heritage of blessings for generations to come. What an exciting prospect!

Women of color can walk in victory over our past failures, wrongs others have done, and even future traps. We can provide blessings for our children, grandchildren, and future generations.

The cost of radical obedience

It will cost us everything we have. It will cost us all of our false gods. It will be extremely uncomfortable.

Much of the pain we are going through right now could be used to thrust us into the kingdom of God. It is there, in the presence of God, that we have fulness of joy. It is there that we have divine protection. If we really understood how good it is living the ways of God, we would rather have the temporary pain of entering that realm than the constant pain of living by the enemy's rules.

God is our Friend, not our enemy. We cannot afford to cooperate with Satan in any way. We will have to give ourselves over to radical obedience to God. We have to jump over to His side without reservation. It may be inconvenient and uncomfortable, but our community has lived enough with the enemy's plan. We need to see what God has to offer. We can't get God's best trying to straddle the fence.

The antibiotic of truth

Believing the lies of the enemy prevents us from obeying God's commands. We have already looked at some of the lies that Satan has put out against women and African Americans in particular. In order to reverse the effects of these lies, we have to give ourselves large doses of truth. Truth refutes lies. We must refuse the lies and accept the truth. It ultimately means accepting all Jesus did for us.

Truth exposes error. Light dispels darkness. Love erases hate, and forgiveness swallows up bitterness. Jesus who is truth, love, light, and forgiveness is ready to set us free and send us forth to be a key to release others from their prisons.

There are several lies the enemy has tried to ingrain in the African American community. The first is that God does not love us as much because of our race. The truth is God loves all people equally. Acts 10:34 says, "God is no respecter of persons. But in every nation he that feareth him, and worketh righteousness, is accepted with him."

Even when He chose to use the Jewish people for His own purposes, He made it clear to them that He did not pick them because they were more in number than others (Deuteroromy 7:7). Jesus also made it clear that His original intentions were to provide His truth to all nations (Matthew 28:19).

After the Day of Pentecost, God proceeded to break down all barriers existing between Jews and other groups. He demonstrated his love to the Black race by supernaturally reaching out to touch the Ethiopian eunuch in Acts 8. In that one act, he demonstrated His provisions were not restricted to one group. A representative of the Black race was one of the first God touched in the New Testament.

God continued to reach out to other groups until it was made abundantly clear His love was for everyone. John 3:16 says, "God so loved the world, that He gave his only begotten Son, that whosoever believeth in Him should not perish, but have everlasting life."

The second lie is that Africans and their descendants are under a permanent curse. Some would say that all who have black skin suffer because of the curse Noah put on his son, Ham. Well, that is just not true. First, Noah did not curse Ham. Take a look at that passage and see who was actually cursed. In Genesis 9:25, it was

Ham's son, Canaan, who was cursed. The curse on the Canaanites was fulfilled when they were wiped out after the children of Israel came into the land of Canaan.

The third lie is people of African descent are inferior to other races. This is simply not true. In fact, Africans were more advanced in the beginning of civilization than other nations. Africans had their turn at ruling the world.

More truth to counteract these lies can be found in the books, *The Black Presence in the Bible and the Table of Nations* by Walter McCray and *Beyond Roots* by Dwight McKissic.

The real destiny of African Americans

The fourth lie, that God cannot use African Americans, is really one of the biggest. In fact, one reason the enemy has fought us so hard is he knows the destiny of African Americans better than we know it.

I believe God wants to use those who have been rejected and oppressed by alcohol, drugs, immorality, and prejudice such as African Americans, women, the young, poor, handicapped, foreign born, etc. to bring healing to this land. These will be trophies of God's grace and love.

A parallel exists between African Americans and Joseph. Joseph, sold into slavery by his brothers, was a slave for a number of years. Even after getting out of slavery, he was lied about, put into prison, and tremendously wronged. But God had a destiny for Joseph all along. Although Satan meant what happen to Joseph for evil, God intended it for good (Genesis 50:20).

Joseph's God-ordained destiny was to be in charge of keeping the people of Israel alive during a time of severe famine. But first Joseph would have to suffer in the depths of his soul. God knew his hardship would produce in him a severe commitment to justice and equity in his eventual role as head of food distribution.

Joseph had to be responsive to the needs of all people, whether poor or not. He had to experience the pits of slavery, attacks on his character, and prison. This worked compassion into him. It also served to uproot pride.

Joseph had a choice. He could choose to be bitter. But he could also choose to forgive those who sold him into slavery and those who abused him in Egypt. He chose the latter, and became a hero in God's "hall of fame."

Somewhere today, there is another Joseph God has chosen for a destiny of greatness. Perhaps this Joseph also dreamed of greatness as a child, excelling in everything. Even after a period of slavery, people demeaned his character and abilities and put him into prison—the prison of drugs, sex, violence, and bitterness.

In spite of that, this Joseph has survived the greatest odds. Perhaps a dream is still in his spirit.

God remembers the dream. He has not forgotten his purposes. Yes, Satan meant all of the injustices for evil, but God had good in mind. God is ready to bring this Joseph out of the prison. God can set him up to be a force for change in His kingdom. God can make him second to none in the throne room of prayer.

Could this Joseph be your child? Your husband? Your friend? You?

We as African Americans, like Joseph, will now have to decide whether we will forgive our African ancestors and whites for the bitter experience of slavery, or sink further into the abyss of bitterness and blame. Our response at this critical time will determine whether we will remain in prison or move into the throne room of the kingdom of God.

As a people we have lived in the wilderness. We know the pitfalls of the wilderness. We have been forced to depend upon Jesus alone. As a people in this nation, the only thing we have had to hang onto has been Jesus.

None of us knows how long it will be until Jesus returns. But Scripture says things will get worse and worse as we approach the last days. African Americans have already gone through many of the rough times that may still be ahead for America. Those who depended upon God—and even some that did not—survived. Who knows? We may be asked to be eyes to lead others in America through the wilderness (Numbers 10:29-31).

It's already happening. A medical physician, Ben Carson, an African American Christian, is an expert in his field. He had a mother who trusted God. When people need his expertise to save the lives of their children, color does not make a lot of difference.The book, *Gifted Hands,* tells about his life.

In many fields, African Americans are excelling. The August 1991 issue of *Ebony* magazine featured highly influential African Americans making a difference in this country. What we have seen so far are just examples of what God can do if we turn around to follow Him completely. Our sons and daughters may hold answers to economic woes, drug addiction, cancer, the environment—any number of problems.

Forgiveness: key to reversing the curse

The love command is the most important command to obey. As we love others, we as African Americans can move to fulfill God's destinies, both in the spiritual and the natural arenas.

We love others by forgiving them of their offences against us. We can obey God by following Matthew 5:44 which says, "Love your enemies, bless them that curse you, do good to them that hate you and pray for them which despitefully use you and persecute you." If we refuse to obey this, we give the enemy the right to continue his torment upon us.

We disobey when we harbor bitterness and unforgiveness, and thereby experience God's curse and not His blessing. To reemphasize when we speak evil of someone, we curse them. When we speak well of someone, we bless them. When evil is spoken about us as a people, we need to bless instead of curse.

"How can we speak well of others when they do such terrible things against us?" We do it because God first forgave us. We do it because to do anything less will take us out of the place of favor with God. Nothing is worth that (Matthew 18:21-35). We do it because we want to reverse the curse on our lives, our families, and our communities.

The way to reverse a curse is the way of the Spirit. The way to continue a curse is to react in the flesh. We're talking about radical obedience to God, because our community needs radical surgery. The question is, do we want to inherit a blessing for our homes and communities or continue in curses?

1 Peter 3:9 clearly tells us how we can inherit the blessing. It says, "Not rendering evil for evil or railing for railing: but contrariwise blessing: knowing that ye are thereunto called, that ye should inherit a blessing." That's it right there. In order to inherit the blessings of God, we have to bless others who don't bless us. Paul did it and instead of being tormented by the enemy, he was feared by demons. When he was reviled, he blessed (1 Corinthians 4:12). This was one of the keys to his authority in the spirit realm.

God wants to put the blessings of Abraham on us (Galatians 3:14). They don't come automatically, not just as a result of being a Christian. They come as the result of radical obedience. They come as a result of living the lifestyle of the Spirit of God. In case you need one more verse to convince you, look at Romans 12:14: "Bless them which persecute you; bless, and curse not."

We have to bless the men who have hurt us, our children who have caused us pain, and whites who have done injustices to us. We do it because we want to receive God's blessings. This may be extremely difficult. People with broken hearts do not bless others easily. However, before we get really hot under the collar, let us just remember God does not ask us to do anything that He will not give us the strength to do. God will perfect His strength in our weakness. God will enable us to do this (2 Corinthians 12:9).

African American women may say, "Yeah, but society's attitudes toward us will not change. Why should we have to do all the forgiving?" One can understand how many may feel this way. African American women have had many negative experiences. But we have to consider who wants things to remain the same. That is not God's plan. God has some new things on His mind. His plan is to turn things around. He can start with African American women.

In order to cooperate with God, we must choose not to cooperate with Satan. Satan is the one who has worked in our lives to bring an entanglement of destruction in our community. He is the one who hates women with a vengeance. He is the only one who wants to see us continue under the curse. We cooperate with him when we refuse to bless others.

African American women are in a unique position to be used of God to avert the increasing judgment on this nation. Praying African American women can use the power of God to stop many of the cycles of division. While being healed of the brokenness of our own hearts, perhaps we can be lights to rescue others from the enemy's tactics they have erroneously followed.

We have the power to forgive all who have offended us in the past and those who continue to offend us today. We have to exercise that power. Our very lives and those of future generations depend upon it. It is not an option for us.

The bondage of lack of forgiveness
It is so important to release forgiveness to everyone the enemy has used against us. God refuses to judge people we insist upon judging. He is a fair God. It's not fair to have two judges. If we would release

others into the hands of God, He'll do a lot better job of dealing with their wrong. And we'll be released of the burden as well.

Our lack of forgiveness is similar to bringing home a thief who stole our car to punish him. Now that we've got him locked up in our spare bedroom, we have to feed, guard, and take care of him. We can't use the room anymore. We can't go out and have fun without worrying if he'll get away. That's a heavy responsibility.

However, if we would just turn him over to the proper authority, justice will be rendered, but not at our expense. God will not only take care of the thief, but will also give us back what he stole and more.

God has many ways of making up for pain. In the example of Job in the Bible, God restored to him two times what was taken. The latter part of Joseph's life made up for the first part. God can make up for years of pain women have suffered. God can make up for pain African Americans have suffered. God can show African American women how to reverse the damage let loose in this earth by the first disobedience of Adam and Eve as we learn to eat from the tree of life—Jesus Christ.

God knows how to bring about equity and justice. We have to let God be God. We have to stop looking to our own strength to pull us up. We have to acknowledge God as our strength and the One who has brought us this far. Yes, the enemy has a plan to destroy us, but God has plans to expand and use us to destroy the enemy. No wonder the enemy is so afraid of us. No wonder he tries so hard to keep us on his side by keeping us under his spell of unforgiveness.

In case you didn't know . . .

For those who do not yet have a right relationship with God, the first step is to accept the gift of God, Jesus' death on the cross, as payment for our sin and receive the power to become a child of God.

Let's broaden our perspective a bit. We must acknowledge the same payment took care of our sins and the sins of others against us. In order to enjoy the fulness of God's forgiveness in this life, it is essential to drop the charges we have against others.

Though Jesus has paid for everybody's sin as far as God is concerned, the law of reaping and sowing is still in effect when it concerns people. When people do unjust things to others, they will reap what they sow in their bodies (Galatians 6:7,8). But as long as we hang on to those who have offended us, it makes it more difficult for them to reap what they have sowed. Accepting Christ's forgiveness for ourselves necessitates releasing others.

Applying Jesus' blood to our past, present and future

As African American women awaken to spiritual reality, walk in the Spirit, and live in oneness with God, loving with His love, the enemy will not be allowed to continue killing, stealing, and destroying our families and cities.

African American women who are members of Christ have to accept some of the responsibility for what has happened in our communities. We have played a part in allowing it. We each have the responsibility to live as godly people to be part of the solution by allowing our bodies to be instruments in the hand of God.

There are some practical things we can do. Christians can participate in the communion table with the knowledge contained in this chapter. The next time we take communion, it would be of great benefit to ask God to give us indications of bitterness or idols in our hearts. As we become aware of false gods or bitterness, we pray the prayer of confession.

But even as we acknowledge the forgiveness of our personal sins, it would be appropriate to also acknowledge the sea of forgiveness covers the sins of our African brothers and sisters that sold us into slavery, the slave masters in our ancestral heritage, ancestors who may have adopted a root of bitterness, parents, bosses, husbands, boyfriends, and anyone who has rejected us.

As we declare to God that we want all of the evil in our family uprooted. we can ask Him for strength to cooperate with His plans. We tell God with His strength we will bless and curse not; we give Him permission to do a "new thing" in us.

Summary
Though we cannot change what has happened in the past, we can change our response to it. We have the power to stop the poison of the past from continuing to affect us and passing on to others.

To stop the poison, we first need to make things right with God. We need to admit He is not the problem. We need to acknowledge our own responsibility. We should ask God to forgive us for believing the accusations against Him.

Second, we need to repent; we need to turn around in our actions and thoughts towards God and others.

Third, we have to turn from the lies that have been ingrained in our minds about God, about men, and about our own worth.

Fourth, we must ask God to heal our broken hearts and to help us sense His presence and His love. Finally, we need to release all those who have been used by the enemy to cause us pain and rejection.

As we remember God has the ability to turn what is meant for evil against us for good, we will also see that God has a destiny for us and uses the suffering to prepare us for it. We will learn to cultivate a relationship with God while we are "going through." As we learn to genuinely forgive those the enemy has used to hurt us, we can use the anger to do battle against the real enemy!

To be great in the throne room of God is to be great in prayer. What could happen if the energies of African American women were spent in prayer? Let's find out. . . .

Chapter 13

What could happen . . . ?

*"For I know the plans I have for you," declares the Lord, "plans to prosper you and not to harm you, plans to give you hope and a future." **Jeremiah 29:11***

Sojourner Truth, Ida B. Wells, Susan B. Anthony, Mary McLeod Bethune, Harriet Tubman, Rosa Parks—all women you may be familiar with —who have fought for freedom. In the struggle for liberty and justice for blacks and women, African American women have played a pivotal role. Though battles have been fought and won on many natural fronts; i.e., voting, riding buses, etc., the war for freedom is still in progress.

Denise, Evelyn, Earnestine, Diane, Pat, Joyce—women you may have not heard of—but who have also fought some battles. They have fought for sons, daughters, husbands, ex-husbands, nephews, fathers, friends, brothers, and mothers. Others have fought against the demons of addiction, infidelity, immorality, rebelliousness, and sickness in the lives of their loved ones. Many have won victories of marriages staying together, salvation, health, and real freedom.

In wrestling the real enemies, many know the fight is not with people (flesh and blood), but with authorities, powers, and rulers of a spiritual nature (Ephesians 6:10). It's time to do battle on a different front. It's time to tell spiritual slave masters, "Let our people go!"

God is now calling women, especially African American women, to take a key role in a spiritual battle. God can reverse the negative effects of "spiritual germs" in our homes, cities, and this nation. . . when African American women use the weapon of prayer.

Contrary to much that we have been conditioned to believe, God loves African American women as much as He loves anyone else. He has unique plans for us no one else can carry out.

What *could* happen if African American women prayed?
Isaiah 43:20 tells us of God's ability, "I give waters in the wilderness, and rivers in the desert, to give drink to my people, my chosen."

Our cities are certainly desert places. But God wants to give us refreshing water. Our cities can become cities of light. It can happen. God can teach us to labor in prayer until this baby of "change" is delivered to our cities.

What could happen if women prayed? If women prayed the way God is calling them to pray, God could send a revival to our land. The revival could prepare the way for a great harvest of souls. As we cry out in prayer for justice, God avenges us of our enemy (Luke 18:3-7). In times of revival, we receive back all the enemy has stolen from us and more (Joel 2:19-27).

Prayer is the most powerful force on earth. Effective prayer dwarfs the power of even nuclear energy. Prayer is the main weapon available to anyone in Christ who wants to see change.

Prayer is the first line of attack against spiritual enemies who would like to see us destroyed. It may not be the only key, but it is certainly the key to the first door. Without it, none of the other keys will work. In the hands of God's people, prayer will bring healing to this land.

It is imperative African American women pray. But the kind of prayer that will bring revival to our cities is not normal prayer. God can use African American women and prayer to start revival. He has brought us to His kingdom for such a time as this. Women are needed to stand in the gap and pray intercessory prayers. We will explore intercession in detail in the next chapter. But to give us a peek, let's look at some Scriptures.

A call to prayer . . .

Exactly what kind of prayer is God calling women to at this time? It is prayer similar to labor. We could call it travail. Paul says in Galatians 4:19, "My little children, of whom I travail in birth again until Christ be formed in you." There is a travail necessary to bring birth and one necessary to bring children to maturity.

Micah 4:10 says, "Be in pain, and labor to bring forth, O daughter of Zion, like a woman in travail: for now shalt thou go forth out of the city, and thou shalt dwell in the field, and thou shalt go to Babylon; there the Lord shall redeem thee from the hand of thine enemies." Also in Isaiah 66:8, we see that, "as soon as Zion travailed, she brought forth her children." Zion represents the church.

. . . for women only

The Scripture that calls women to prayer is Jeremiah 9:17-21:

> Thus saith the Lord of hosts, Consider ye, and call for the mourning women that they may come; and send for cunning women, that they may come: And let them make haste, and take up a wailing for us, that our eyes may run down with tears, and our eyelids gush out with waters. For a voice of wailing is heard out of Zion, How are we spoiled! We are greatly confounded, because we have forsaken the land, because our dwellings have cast us out. Yet hear the word of the Lord, O ye women, and let your ear receive the word of his mouth, and teach your daughters wailing, and every one her neighbor lamentation. For death is come up into our windows, and is entered

into our palaces, to cut off the children from without, and the young men from the streets.

In this passage, we note prayer going beyond making requests. "Let us make haste" indicates an urgency. "A wailing," "tears," and "eyelids gushing out with waters", all indicate great intensity.The words uttered, too, are different, as in vs.19: "How are we spoiled! We are greatly confounded, because we have forsaken the land, because our dwellings have cast us out." The women who are praying are admitting their wrong.They are praying the prayer of confession.

Verse 21 tells us why there is a need for such urgency, intensity, and confession. "Death is come up into our windows, and is entered into our palaces, to cut off the children from without, and the young men from the streets. . . . " Sounds a lot like our urban areas today, doesn't it?

Cocaine, alcohol, promiscuous lifestyles, suicide, violence, the New Age movement, gangs, homosexuality, and much more are swallowing up our youth, our children. Loneliness, despair, hopelessness, and debt are doing their damage in our families.

Is death coming into our windows to cut off the children? Have you read in the papers about little girls murdered in their own homes, AIDS capturing more victims, suicide threatening to take away more young lives, abortions taking thousands daily? Women, we need to respond to this call to prayer NOW.

Do we need to wait before we take up wailing? When is enough enough? What will it take before we make haste to pray with an intensity that is beyond our normal supplications?

These are our sons, nephews, daughters, nieces, granddaughters, grandsons, and neighbors. This is the future generation. Perhaps the next Mary McLeod Bethune or Ben Kinchlow is among them. Do we sit idly by and let them be picked off one by one?

The call is going out now to mourning women and wise (cunning) women to take up a wailing that our children might be spared. The call is going out to women who are willing to pray with an intensity beyond the norm, willing to leave the familiar and traditional behind. Desperate circumstances call for drastic measures, maybe even some emotional involvement.

Prayer is a large part of the ministry in the home. As African American mothers seek God in prayer, they will train their children by the wisdom God gives. Through prayer, women will take authority over the enemy as he tries to bring his wares into the lives of their children. As women stay close to God, many will be warned of the enemy's plans before they come to pass.

Just recently, a friend of mine woke up early in the morning and was impressed to pray for her daughter who was away at camp. Both she and her husband prayed, taking authority over the enemy's plans. A couple of days later, her daughter was spared serious injury, even death as the truck she was riding in turned over and slid across the highway. Not only was her child safe, but three registered nurses were in the car right behind the accident and a police car was a couple of lanes over. The fire department came within minutes. By being obedient and sensitive, this mother participated in reversing the plans of destruction for her family.

Women need to pray children away from the plans and traps of the enemy and into God's hands for God's use and glory. Women are keepers and women are also keys. Yes, at this time, this critical time, prayer—the key to the front door—is needed.

Another mother shared with me how she prayed specifically that her daughter would be kept pure until her wedding night. God honored the prayer. Our young people hardly have a chance unless they have those who will intercede for them.

African American women can begin to come together in corporate settings to pray for issues in our cities. They can also join together to pray and fast for relatives who are still under bondage. Together they can pray and strategize to release others from spiritual prisons.

Christians even from different denominations can come together, refusing to let those differences deter them from the work of prayer. Though they may still believe differently or even have different ways of praying, they will avoid offending each other and agree to work for that which is most important—change in our homes and communities.

Summary

What could happen if African American women prayed? The power of God could be unleashed. A woman who learns the proper use of prayer is an instrument of righteousness. In this way, she offers her body as a sacrifice unto the Lord. In this way, she pours out God's unconditional love upon others.

Many talk of prayer, but there is a privilege in prayer that few enter. Women of color need to be thrust into the next level of praying for others—intercession. Though we were briefly introduced to it in this chapter, that is the focus of the next chapter.

Chapter 14

Ministry of intercession

*And I sought for a man [woman] among them, that should make up the hedge,
and stand in the gap before me for the land, that I should not destroy it: but I
found none. **Ezekiel 22:30***

One of the keys to the power of the New Testament Church is
the emphasis placed on prayer. Acts 6:4 tells us the first
apostles wanted to be relieved of their duties so that they could give
themselves continually to intercession—prayer and the ministry of
the Word. It is significant that prayer was mentioned first. Prayer was
the priority.

In the battle to breathe new life into the African American community, we must move to a level beyond that of praying only for
ourselves. The deepening of our ministry begins as we move to pray
consistently and effectively for others.

We can see throughout the epistles in the New Testament the
mention of prayer and the time spent in prayer. For the early
believers prayer was key. In most of the letters from Paul, he
mentioned he was praying for them. He mentioned in Colossians
4:12 another servant, Epaphras, always labored fervently for them

in prayers. The first century church tapped into a power of which current believers know very little.

The ministry of intercession

Intercession is the highest form of ministry. In fact, Jesus Himself now carries out the ministry of intercession on our behalf (Hebrews 7:25). It is one of the most powerful tools given to God's people for accomplishing change in the world. And historically, women have played a significant role.

The ministry of intercession is bringing the world to Christ by talking to the Father about men (prayer), and is bringing Christ to the world by talking to men about and for the Father (Word ministry). Those who are effective are able to take authority over the plans, strategies, lies, and works of evil spirits so that mankind can really know and understand the Father.

This nation is starving for true intercessors. Those who have been trained to intercede for others are needed to bring those skills in the fight for our cities. Those who would stand in the gap and make up the hedge are desperately needed to avert the attacks of our spiritual enemies.

Intercessory prayer in our homes and cities will bring change. Yes, African American women have been called to be intercessors.

God intends us to be equipped intercessors, using the weapon of intercessory prayer. Many people think they are interceding when they pray for someone other than themselves. That is true to an extent, but there is so much more involved.

God can shape us into people who only ask what is in the heart of God. These are friends of God. These are people who hear God's heartbeat. These are the true intercessors. They are not born, they are made. Boot camp breeds true intercessors. Intercession is a ministry taught to us in the trenches of life.

An intercessor will eventually be able to pray with the effectiveness of Elijah."Elijah was a man subject to like passions as we are, and he prayed earnestly that it might not rain: and it rained not on the earth by the space of three years and six months. And he prayed again, and the heaven gave rain, and the earth brought forth her fruit" (James 5:17,18).

The person skilled in intercession is a specialist who can also rescue others. Prayer is part of spiritual warfare according to Ephesians 6:18. If people trained to use a weapon would always hit the target, it would make more sense to have ten such people than a thousand others.

It would be futile to try to gather a thousand people to pray when 99.99% of them cannot even get a prayer through. A mere 12 that have grown in the area of intercessory prayer could turn a city upside down.

Just as it would be foolish to invite untrained people to participate in a war, it does not make sense to use skilled people without the weapon they have been trained to use. As in every skill, practice makes perfect. There are already plenty of opportunities in the lives of most African American women to practice the skill of intercession. With increased practice, one is being trained to become one of the specialists God will be able to use to hit the target every time.

Everybody can be an intercessor. It is not restricted to a special class of people. God is looking for intercessors to stand in the gap. The call is going out for those who will stand in the gap on the behalf of families, churches, neighborhoods, cities, and nation.

An intercessor has a very important role in the body of Christ. The prayers of intercession make up for weaknesses in the body. The function of intercession is to provide blood to different areas of the body in order to remove waste material from cells, provide nutrients, and bring white blood cells to fight germs. By standing in the gap and praying the prayer of confession for the body of Christ, intercessors bring cleansing and restoration.

God wants people to remind Him of what He said He would do. Isaiah 62:6,7 says: "On your walls, O Jerusalem, I have appointed watchmen; all day and all night they will never keep silent. You who remind the Lord, take no rest for yourselves; and give Him no rest until He establishes and makes Jerusalem a praise in the earth."

The prayer which hits the target every time is one in which the intercessor asks the Father the prayers He asks her to pray. An intercessor typically does not decide what she prays. Her prayers are unique because they are the ones the heavenly Father has asked her to pray. An intimacy with the Father is essential to this lifestyle of prayer.

When God wants to do something, He alerts His intercessors. They ask Him what He tells them to ask and then He has the legal right to do what He wanted to do in the first place.

When the enemy comes to accuse God of interfering with the affairs of man, the record is pulled out of intercessors asking. He tells the enemy, "Oh, I only did it because my children asked me. I respond when asked. That was the agreement." The enemy is mad. He can't say anything else. God rests His case.

We should see very clearly why the enemy hates the ministry of intercession. It's a power packed ministry. The enemy does not mind people praying, but He detests people praying the prayers God asks them to pray. The enemy would rather have 1,000 preachers and teachers than one true intercessor. He desperately fights the making of an intercessor. But as we have already seen, the Father uses the very fiery attacks of the enemy to purify the intercessor.

Living on two levels

An intercessor lives in two realms. In the physical, an intercessor lives on earth. An intercessor does all of the physical functions this world requires. Physically, an intercessor also uses her body as an instrument of righteousness. She uses her tongue to bless, teach, train, and encourage others. This is the ministry of the Word.

The spiritual realm is the second home of the intercessor. She is as much at home in the spiritual realm as in the physical realm. She has already passed through enemy territory to make her abode in the heavenly kingdom. She has labored to enter into that rest. From this position she can function with authority over evil spirits. She does it in relationship with her Father, not independently.

The intercessor knows she is not her own, but has been bought with a price. When someone is in desperate need of prayer, God knows He can bring this person into her life. He may allow this person to grievously offend her, knowing she will understand that the offending party is putting in a prayer request. Instead of becoming offended, she will go into her prayer closet.

The intercessor practices the following Scripture: "But I say to you which hear, Love your enemies, do good to them which hate you. Bless them that curse you, and pray for them which despitefully use you" (Luke 6:27,28).

An intercessor takes authority over the enemy and his plans. She is familiar enough with the enemy's tactics and traps that she can go back to rescue others without falling into the traps herself.

Contrary to popular belief, God's main way of operating in the earth is not by preaching, teaching, or laying on of hands. These are important. A knowledge of the Word is needed for her to know what to pray. But God's main way of getting things done on earth is through prayer.

We see an example of this in the life of Daniel. He realized from the Scriptures it was time for the captives to go back to Israel. Upon understanding this, he then sought God for it to happen (Daniel 9:1-19). God did not just do it, but rather He made a servant of His aware this was what He wanted to happen. The servant asked Him and God did it. This is God's method.

This is seen in the New Testament as well. Although Jesus' coming had been prophesied many times in the Old Testament, at the proper time God once again used someone to ask Him to bring it to pass. It did not happen without the prayers of humans. I believe the intercessory ministry of Anna the prophetess was specifically for that purpose. In partnership with God, she participated in one of the greatest events in history:

> And there was also a prophetess, Anna, the daughter of Phanuel, of the tribe of Aser. She was very old; she had lived with her husband seven years after her marriage, and then was a widow until she was eighty-four. She never left the temple, but worshiped night and day, fasting and praying. Coming up to them at that moment, she gave thanks to God and spoke about the child to all who were looking forward to the redemption of Jerusalem. (Luke 2:36-38 NIV)

Another example is the coming of the Holy Spirit on the day of Pentecost. Jesus had already told His disciples in John 14 and in Acts 1:8 about the Spirit's coming. Acts 1:14 says the disciples and the women were continually in prayer those ten days in the upper room.

Ever wonder what they were praying about? I personally believe they were praying back to God what Jesus had told them He wanted to happen. Acts 2 was the answer to the prayers.

You might argue it would have happened anyway even if they did not ask. Yet, James tells us in chapter 4:2 we have not because we ask not. God gives us His Word on a situation. We take His Word and ask Him to fulfill it, then God acts. It is my conviction God acts only in response to our prayers based on His Word, not just because His Word says it.

Other aspects of intercession

The intercessor is being anchored into God at the same time she is being detached from her circumstances and the expectations of others. We do not have to continue to act out of self-preservation, fear, inferiority, and all of the old ways. As we learn to let God be God, He proves Himself as our provider, protector, revenge, defender, healer, anchor, and peace.

The highest level of intercessory prayer is praying for one's enemies. Some may pray for other people and others may pray for the purposes of God, but the intercessor specialist has learned to pray for those who have despitefully used or offended her. By passing through the hardest love preparation, she is guaranteed a hearing when she prays. She is the one who can clearly hear the purposes of God.

Intercessors can be uniquely used of God to bring God's will to earth by bringing requests to God, but also by speaking to men on God's behalf. The intercessor will say to man the things God directs. These words are not her own. They are from the Spirit. They are as the oracles of God (1 Peter 4:11). And they can accomplish more than a hundred sermons given in human wisdom.

Life flows from her, even as death is at work in her. The pain and suffering has brought death to her flesh. Daily, she dies to her own thoughts, ideas, rights, abilities, and strength. She does not mind death to self as long as the life of Jesus is ministered to the ones she touches (2 Corinthians 4:12).

Let's look at racism as an example. An intercessor who sees evidence of racism in her boss who is also a professing Christian, does not become bitter and write him off. Instead she intercedes by asking God to have mercy on her brother in Christ as she realizes oneness in the body of Christ is being hindered. *An intercessor is one who not only sees beneath the surface, but also is willing to make up for the lack.*

Instead of using her tongue for slander, gossip, or criticism, she weeps. She asks God to give the person opportunity to repent. She asks God to forgive the person and provide spiritual understanding.

The woman God uses has to agree with God about the ability of the blood of Jesus to cover the wrongs of others. She lets go of bitterness and resentment. She prays for and does good to individuals who have been used by Satan, either against her or against the cause of Christ.

In most cases the ministry of intercession is hidden. It's not an open ministry. People do not have to know who is involved in the ministry of intercession. Sometimes visibility will hinder its effectiveness. When women intercessors want recognition, the ministry will immediately diminish from the purposes of God. Any exalting needed will be done by God. Intercessors will even have to prevent others from trying to exalt them.

The rewards of being an intercessor are excellent

The rewards of intercessory prayer cannot compare to the suffering. Just as medical students voluntarily go through a lot of pain and struggle to achieve their goals, the intercessor should look on her boot camp in the same way. But when it is over, she hardly remembers the pain of boot camp. The benefits of her new job are so splendid.

Because she has learned to seek God's kingdom and His righteousness first, the intercessor has a right to inherit all of the promises of God for blessings, healing, prosperity, peace, and protection (Matthew 6:33). God adds all things, her needs are met. As she has delighted herself in God, she has the desires of her heart (Psalm 37:4).

This does not mean her life is filled with an abundance of material possessions. Sometimes she doesn't desire that much. In fact, the relationship with her Father means much more to her than material possessions. But if she needs something to get His work done, she gets it. If she needs more to be able to give to others, she has it.

The intercessor is able to even give up her rights, even rights to God's promises for the sake of the gospel (1 Corinthians 9). She understands the blessings God wants to give are for His whole Body and not just individuals. She doesn't mind deferring her participation in these blessings in order to bring others into the same. She gladly lays her life down on behalf of others.

An intercessor knows the plans of the enemy for herself and her family before they take place. We see this in the life of the prophet Elisha and the Apostle Paul, who were some of the great intercessors of old (2 Kings 6:9-17 and Acts 27:10).

At times, the intercessor can use the knowledge to avert the plans of the enemy; other times, she uses it to prepare herself for the attack if it is the purpose of her Father to go through it. In either case, as a friend of God, there are few surprises.

Life is dynamic and joyous for the intercessor. She knows in God's presence is fulness of joy (Psalm 16:11). The fellowship with her Father is precious. His approval is worth more than the approval of the whole world. She can rejoice when persecuted for the sake of the gospel. God directly intervenes in her affairs. He shows her His love in tangible ways.

Each day for the intercessor brings the possibility of yet another difficult assignment. She may get an assignment to love an obstinate person. The benefits will get the intercessor through difficult assignments. She will continue to receive assignments to love difficult people. That's her job, the purpose of her training. Perhaps someone will yell at her because of the way she is driving. Perhaps she hears someone on her job is talking about her behind her back. Perhaps her daughter's teacher is giving her child a hard time. These are all prayer assignments. In obeying the Scripture, she prays for these people.

The intercessor would never risk frustrating God's plan by refusing to pray for the persons offending her. Speaking against or ignoring them is totally out of the question. God would then have to bring them into someone else's life while working on her until she learns the strategy.

If she encounters a particularly difficult situation, other women can join her. As the assignments progress beyond the home, two or more join together to intercede for wider circles. The ministry of intercession is best carried out in conjunction with others.

Some people, because of their own wrong choices and the place the enemy has in their lives, are in need of the blessings of God. God has so arranged things to bring those persons into her life to get blessings and prayer according to the spiritual laws given in Luke 6:27 and 28.

Members of her own family may be reaping serious infection by "spiritual germs." Her intercession can be used to bring them to repentance and a right relationship with God.

The ministry of intercession is a calling for everyone. The ministry of intercession is the fulfillment of the purposes for which humankind was made. It's for everybody who names the name of Christ. All of us will eventually have opportunity to enter this ministry if we continue to live on this earth.

Intercession: a ministry for African American women

The ministry of intercession as defined in this chapter is desperately needed. It wouldn't take many intercessors of this caliber to change our cities. It wouldn't take many cities experiencing this change to change our nation. Many are interceding for others in powerful ways. They have prepared the way for the unique intercessor that is now needed.

Fortunately, God is an equal opportunity employer when it comes to recruiting intercessors. He does not discriminate according to gender or race. In fact, He is seeking minorities. African American women are needed in this great work and are being actively sought after to take intercession farther than it has ever been.

The African American woman is not better than others. Since going through fiery furnaces is a prerequisite to forging this precious ministry, many women of color already have the workings of pain, suffering, and trials in their lives.

When it is time to determine the destiny of a criminal, the victim has to decide whether or not to press charges. Women and African Americans have been victims of gross injustices in this country. African American women are in a unique position to ask for mercy in place of judgment for fellow members of the body of Christ from the past and the present. Through intercession, African American women can release others into the hands of the Judge of all the earth who will do right.

Through intercession, African American women can be keys to positive change in this nation. God has chosen them as vessels of intercession.

Summary
A different caliber of intercession is needed today. African American women are able to take up this assignment. If African American women would just exchange all of the suffering, all of the pain, disappointments and receive the glory due them, they could be used mightily in God's kingdom in praying for others. The ministry of intercession is forged in painful fires, but has great rewards for those who enter in.

Yes, many African American women who are called to serve as specialists are going through boot camp. It's hard. But we can gather strength to help us press on through the trials and pain, receiving the equipping needed to smash the gates of hell.

Women have a unique opportunity to become intercessors for families. A woman intercessor will intercede for her children from the time they are born. African American women also have the unique potential in being intercessors for this nation. An African American female intercessor can be a powerful tool in the hands of our mighty God.

Perhaps women will begin to run to God instead of resisting Him as they understand what God has been doing. Perhaps as African American women begin to take on the ministry of intercession, our families, neighborhoods, churches, cities, and nation will experience change.

"Weeping may endure for a night, but joy comes in the morning" (Psalm 30:5). It is a new day for African American women. We have suffered much, but God is ready to give us the glory of His presence.

As we pursue intimacy with our Lord Jesus Christ, we will experience the fullness of joy that comes with His presence. As we draw nigh to God, He will draw nigh to us (James 4:8). As His glory shines upon us, we will be able to fully function in the ministry of intercession.

Different kinds of prayers must be prayed to see some real change in our communities and nation. We introduced intercession as a means to bring God's mercy into the life of people who are away from God. Intercession is so critical if we want to see real change.

Chapter 15

Covering prayer

Above all, love each other deeply, because love covers a multitude of sins.
1 Peter 4:8, NIV

As noted in the chapter on the baptism of fire, when we pray for ourselves, God also allows the fires of testing to come. We have compared it to going through "boot camp"—a tough, rigorous training that will prepare us for a greater and deeper ministry.

Just as the personal prayer of confession to God was one of the first prayers we needed to exercise in our own healing, so the *covering prayer* is prayer of confession for others. This prayer is vital for us to use on our loved ones, friends, and fellow members in God's family who have gone astray. The covering prayer combines the prayer of confession, the SOS prayer, and asking prayer for someone other than ourselves.

As we have said before, sin puts a hole in our armor and attracts the enemy to our lives. God hates to see His children uncovered and away from the protection of the blood of Jesus. He has given us all things pertaining to life and godliness (2 Peter 1:3). He has given us instructions to live a victorious life. He has provided His own strength to live that life through us. Yet, He has also given us a free will by which we can choose to leave His protection, and has provided confession as a means to move back when we wander off.

In spite of God's provisions, we still can be deceived. So God has instituted a way for other members of the Body of Christ to provide a "covering" for each other. At times, all of us could benefit by this covering. It allows those who are strong in certain areas to cover other's weaknesses in those areas.

Now only personal confession and repentance can get someone back under the full protection of God. But another person can, through the covering prayer, deflect the fiery darts of the devil.

The covering is a temporary measure. It is for a period of time until the person deals with his or her own sin. Once you are convicted and repent of your wicked ways, you no longer need the covering.

When you have become consistent in seeing prayer work in your own life, God will give you a chance to work your prayers into the lives of others. He might have you intervene on someone else's behalf to help them avoid judgment. He might have you pray and fast on behalf of someone who is in the clutches of a sin "stronghold." As you learn to obey the Scriptural admonition to bear the infirmities of the weak, God will help you positively affect the lives of others (Romans 15:1).

God lets us see the weaknesses of others so we may cover them in prayer. In the past, I probably thought I saw them so I could feel superior and gossip. God exposed the enemy's plan in my life. When we follow the enemy's plan we grieve God. Many Christians remain weak because others have not cooperated with God's plan to cover their weaknesses.

Who needs covering?

Young saints especially need this kind of covering. They do not have the skills to operate successfully in the realm of spiritual battle. Just as in the natural realm we provide a little extra protection for babies and young children because of their immaturity and lack of experience, so in the spiritual realm, those who are older in the Lord will often have to cover the younger.

Others are seriously handicapped due to a blow that has affected them emotionally. A person who has a broken heart is somewhat of a spiritual cripple. This person needs prayer for her broken heart, which can sometimes serve to hinder her ability to stay under the protecting arms of God.

Others have a blind spot in their lives. Even the most spiritual among us have weak, unseen places. These are the places others have to stand for us.

Most Christians in this country are taught that following a list of do's and don'ts produces spiritual growth. This is simply not true. Many Christians trying to follow the lists are still immature after many years .

The number of years that a person has been a Christian has nothing to do at all with whether they need covering. Many people have not really had anyone to disciple them in the spiritual realm.

What a person knows intellectually has nothing to do with spiritual knowledge. We cannot judge based on outer appearances such as education or the ability to speak well. We have to judge righteously.

We all have holes. We cover each other's sins by praying God's protection over each other's holes. We cover by asking God to deal with the other person in those areas. We cover by refusing to discuss it with others. We cover by standing in the gap as Nehemiah did and even confessing the sins of others (1:6). We cover by asking God to give the other person life (1 John 5:16).

Please cover me

Let's use an illustration here. Picture that you are part of a battlefield with armored soldiers. You see that the soldier next to you has a hole in his armor. Right at the time you see the hole, you also observe the soldier taking careful aim at the enemy. He's about ready to blast him. What should you do?

First, look at what you should not do. The battle is very intense. Everybody is needed. If any one soldier is taken out of the battle, it becomes more dangerous for everyone. This would not be a good time to distract him to tell him about the hole.

Neither do you want to point the hole out to everybody around you. That will only alert the enemy and make it easier for him to attack the perceived "weak spots."

What you do want to do is to assist the person until you see a more appropriate time to deal with the problem. But now, in the heat of the battle, the only thing you want to do is to cover the hole.

Though you do not go immediately to tell him and the other soldiers about the hole, you are not ignoring it. If you have seen the hole, you also have a responsibility to cover it. By doing so, you keep a soldier on the field. Love covers a multitude of sins (1 Peter 4:8).

The time may come when you will have to confront the issue. Sometimes God will deal with the person personally or even through someone else as you just pray. You may not even get involved. But sometimes, you will be asked to speak the truth in love.

There is a place for godly confrontation. There is a place for tough love. Love does not overlook the sin in others, letting them slide down the road of destruction without warning.

In confronting, however, timing is key. We should not confront until we have covered. Covering will help us confront in love. Most of our confronting is probably done out of a critical spirit if we have not learned to cover.

We should also not confront until we have "taken the log out of our own eyes" and examined ourselves. It is easy to see the faults of others and ignore our own.

God's Word tells us to look to ourselves when we restore another. That would involve the searchlight prayer. Can you imagine how clean we would be if we took each chance that we saw fault in others to go to God for personal cleansing?

The ultimate goal of covering

The covering prayer is not as passive as some might think. It triggers the restorative work of the Holy Spirit and paves the way for confrontation and counsel by those who are living godly, Spirit-controlled lives. It provides a temporary "patch" until the full work of restoration, which involves personal confession by the offending party, can take place.

Nehemiah 1:6 and Ezra 9:7 are each accounts of one person standing in the gap, praying the prayer of confession for others. Take a look: "Let Thine ear now be attentive and Thine eyes open to hear the prayer of Thy servant which I am praying before Thee now, day and night, on behalf of the sons of Israel Thy servants, confessing the sins of the sons of Israel which we have sinned against Thee; I and my father's house have sinned" (Nehemiah 1:6).

The next prayer of confession, "Since the days of our fathers to this day we have been in great guilt, and on account of our iniquities we, our kings and our priests have been given into the hand of the kings of the lands, to the sword, to captivity, and to plunder and to open shame" (Ezra 9:7).

Along with covering prayer assignments God gives us in our homes and among friends, we can also use this prayer as indicated in the Scripture above to confess the sins of our "fathers" and fellow members of the family of God in this country—yes, those connected to us by the Spirit who were and are wrong in their attitude and behavior to our ancestors and us by not discerning us as fellow members in the body of Christ because of the color of our skin or gender of our body.

Many among the people of God were and are still under an evil influence of not discerning the body correctly. This is the cause of weakness, sickness, and premature death among the people of God in spite of the fact of the stripes of Jesus as a provision for healing. That will not be fully realized as long as this evil prevails among members of the body.

African American women hold a unique place in God's family to confess those sins, past, present and future until God moves to bring conviction and a revelation of the oneness of His body.

Summary

Be assured: we will receive assignments for covering others as we continue to learn what it means to be wholly God's. God will be training and using us at the same time.

The covering prayer is designed to hold off the attacks of the enemy temporarily. This is part of being involved in the lives of others.

God has a destiny for African American women. They have a very important role to play in the healing of this nation. We must press on so that the original plan of God can be fulfilled: the defeat of God's enemy by men *and* women committed to Him.

The final section brings together all we have discussed to show how women of color have been chosen to impact this nation as they bring healing to their families and communities.

In the next chapter, we'll look at ways God uses women. Though in the spirit, there is no distinction between male and female in the healing of our communities, women have some unique assignments in ministry.

Section four: Putting it together

Chapter 16

Women's place

But God hath chosen the foolish things of the world to confound the wise; and God hath chosen the weak things of the world to confound the things which are mighty; and base things of the world, and things which are despised, hath God chosen, yea, and things which are not, to bring to nought things that are: that no flesh should glory in his presence. 1 Corinthians 1:27-30

Prayer is foundational. It is an awesome privilege. If prayer were the only key in our hands, it would be more than enough. But God has given us something more. There is an additional key to be used in ministry roles and to influence families and communities.

The keys are really two sides of the same coin. They are the Word and prayer. In order for an individual to be a woman of prayer, she has to be a woman of the Word. She must be balanced, using both sides of her spiritual brain. The Word of God is the basis for all prayer. Prayer is the key for every purpose God has for women.

The prayers of women of the Word are the secret weapons God has chosen for such a time as this. The woman of prayer and the Word can be a powerhouse in destroying the kingdom of Satan. As noted in the discussion on the ministry of intercession, an intercessor stands in the gap, talking to God on the behalf of men and also speaks to man on God's behalf. This chapter explores how God uniquely uses the prayers of women in His kingdom. It also examines ways in which God uses a woman's tongue filled with God's Word.

It cannot be overemphasized how important women are to the plan of God. Women have been lied to for so long many hesitate to come forth and take their places. Other women try to get involved in things that are not for them. They know God has called them to ministry, but are not sure how to do the work of the ministry.

Women in the purposes of God

God uses women, not to the exclusion of men, but beside men— husbands, brothers, sons, fathers, or fellow members in God's family. God uses couples, couples taking dominion over their world and cooperating in tasks God gives. Many women who are waiting to enter "the ministry" are already surrounded with ministry opportunities.

God gave both man and woman the task to have dominion over the earth, over the fish of the sea, and over every living thing. He wanted them to complement and compensate for each other. His original plan was for them to work together as equals. That plan has a renewed hope as a result of Jesus' work on the cross.

God is now bringing women to the purposes He had ordained from the beginning. It is imperative women pray. This is not only the means by which we will stop the aggression of the enemy on the human race and storm hell's gates, but it is the means God uses to bring women into His original order.

We have examined the animosity Satan has against women and took a look at the seed of woman that God promised would defeat Satan. We also know that seed was Jesus. It was promised that "the seed would bruise his head." Colossians 2:15 assures us that,

"Having spoiled principalities and powers, he [Jesus] made a show of them openly, triumphing over them in it."

Women, symbols of the bride of Christ

Satan knows he is defeated. But as long as he can lie and trick others into believing that he is not defeated, he'll carry out his plans under the cover of deception. The bride of Christ, the church, has been left here to spread the good news of the enemy's defeat. She has been given the power and authority to enforce what Christ did on the cross.

The only way Satan has been able to continue his work is because a woman—the church—has been sleeping on her job. Now when she wakes up, Satan will no longer be able to carry out his work so effectively. In fact, the church has the privilege of cooperating with Jesus "until all His enemies are made His footstool" (Hebrews 10:13).

Let's take a look at a promise in Genesis. "Thou art our sister, be thou the mother of thousands of millions, and let thy seed possess the gate of those which hate them" (Genesis 24:60). This was a blessing that Isaac's wife, Rebekah, received. Isaac was a type of Christ and Rebekah, his wife, was a type of the church; this promise is therefore for the Church as well. Jesus confirmed it in Matthew 16:18. He said that the gates of hell would not prevail against the church.

In Ephesians 5:21-23, we see the wife is a type of the church. So beginning in the home and extending into the community, women have been given the assignment of defeating the plan of the enemy. This is women's special place.

Even as women symbolize the bride of Christ, they have some unique roles in God's kingdom. Just as Satan targeted women to orchestrate the fall, God also has targeted women to orchestrate bringing the return of humankind to the original plan of God.

Women as "birthers" and "nurturers"

Though there are no female/male distinctions in the spiritual realm, God's Spirit manifests itself through women in unique ways. Much of what God does through women in the ministry of His kingdom correlates to what they have been uniquely fitted to do in the physical realm.

For example, only women can give birth. Women are also used by God as vehicles to birth new spiritual movements into the earth.

But women do not do it alone. Just as conception does not take place without the seed from a man, likewise the birthing of God's will by women requires cooperation with like-minded Christian men. Instead of competition, there needs to be a harmony that recognizes the unique contribution of both men and women.

To use another analogy, just as intimacy is required as a prerequisite to physical birth, so spiritual intimacy with the Lord Jesus is required for God's will to manifest itself in the lives of women.

Let's take the analogy a little further. Not only has God uniquely designed women to give birth to children in the natural realm, but He has also fitted them to feed and nurture children, especially in the early years. The mother's milk is the perfect food for a baby. Women have a mothering instinct that serves to care for, protect, and defend those who are unable to provide for themselves.

This is also true in the spiritual realm. God uses women to care for and protect the new movements that He brings forth. He also uses women to care for and protect new spiritual babies.

Women are specially equipped for nurturing physically, emotionally, and spiritually. If she is a mother, the most important nurturing is to those in her home. If she is not, she still has plenty of opportunities to minister to troubled young people suffering from homes dominated by drugs or otherwise dysfunctional. Children who do not have godly mothers in their own homes are in need of surrogate (substitute) mothers who will nurture them.

The process by which children become functioning adults comes largely from the influence of women, mothers, grandmothers and others. Timothy, in the Bible, is a key example of the results of the spiritual nurture received from women in his life (2 Timothy 1:5).

Many women who do not have young children are called upon to nurture other children through neighborhood Bible clubs, Sunday School and camp.

Women as keepers at home

The third important role for women—right up there with birthing and nurturing—is to bring forth and provide a loving foundation for future generations. Titus 2:4,5 alludes to the importance of women loving their children and being keepers of their homes.

The family was instituted in the garden of Eden as fundamental to healthy life. The woman was instituted as key to the family unit. It is still true that the hand that rocks the cradle rules the world.

Barbara Beeler writes of the role and place for women as keepers of the family in an article entitled "The Keepers." In the article she gave illustrations from the animal kingdom, showing how females protect their young, train them to fly, teach, and give comfort.

How does a mother participate in dominion over the earth? She does it by exercising authority over the plans of the enemy. She keeps her family protected from the enemy. She takes authority in the spiritual realm.

And let us not forget every woman has a role in the lives of a number of family members, whether as sister, aunt, grandmother, daughter, or niece.

The enemy is having a field day with our youth. Sometimes your days—or even your years—may seem wasted with sins and mistakes. Well, Jesus can give those years back to us. God promised in Joel 2:25 to "restore of the years that the locust hath eaten, the cankerworm, and the caterpillar, and the palmerworm." Every woman can be used of God to defend young ones from the enemy through prayers, attention, instruction, and nurturing.

Finally, let us not forget mothers need "mothering" too. Women who take care of mothers in matters both spiritual and practical help them to better nurture their families. Sometimes a woman's ministry will be to pray for sisters, brothers, cousins, and friends so they may become the parents children need.

Submission is key to the power of influence

Submission is one of those "dirty words" for women. The author of a book about submission tells that when she announces the topic of submission to her audience, women visibly stiffen. The book, *Liberated Through Submission: The Essence of Power*, by P. B. Wilson, an African American author, is recommended reading. The Bible gives us a different view of submission than the world would have us believe. The power of submission is found in the following:

> Wives, in the same way be submissive to your husbands so that, if any of them do not believe the word, they may be won over without words by the behavior of their wives when they see the purity and reverence of your lives. Your beauty should not come from outward adornment, such as braided hair and the wearing of gold jewelry and fine clothes. Instead, it should be that of your inner self, the unfading beauty of a gentle and quiet spirit, which is of great worth in God's sight. For this is the way the holy women of the past who put their hope in God used to make themselves beautiful. They were submissive to their own husbands, like Sarah, who obeyed Abraham and called him her master. You are her daughters if you do what is right and do not give way to fear. (1 Peter 3:1-6)

Our submission to God is often reflected in our attitudes towards those in authority in our lives: fathers, husbands, bosses, employers, or church leaders. Do we criticize, murmur, complain, resent, or pray for those in authority over us?

A woman's dependency upon God is not the same as depending on her husband's spiritual growth. We are each individually responsible to God for our own spiritual growth. Some women will cease seeking to grow spiritually because their husbands are not moving along fast enough. They do not want to get too far ahead.

The position of the man as head of the wife is not in relationship to spiritual growth. A woman can never use her husband as an excuse on the day of judgment for laxity in her spiritual walk.

The man will be responsible for the direction of his home in practical matters. The husband is head of his wife in this way. A man will also take responsibility for whom the home yields service. Men should declare as Joshua declared, "as for me and my house, we will serve the Lord."

A woman, however, can certainly choose to serve the Lord on her own even if her household is not serving God. Though it is easier for a man to steer the direction of his home towards God, women can influence the husband to come to the same decision through godly submission.

Obedience to God in the area of submission is vitally important if we are to use the powerful tool of influence in our homes. Men who are not submitted to God can learn submission from their wives.

Children can learn about submission to authority from their mothers' example. As was previously stated in the chapter, " Bitter roots," many African Americans move from the protecting hand of God by violating the principle of proper attitudes towards authority.

What are the real issues that cause us difficulty in obeying God in the area of submitting to our husbands and other authorities? Is it really because many men are tyrants, chauvinistic, selfish and abusive? Granted this is often the case. We do not want to minimize the difficulty in living under such ungodly circumstances. The enemy has broken many women's hearts at the hand of those with positions of authority.

The real issue, however, is not one of trust in a fallen man who is being used as a tool in Satan's hand. The real issue is one of faith in a good God who is bigger than the devil. The question is not whether our men can hear from God and lead us correctly, the question is whether our God is big enough to make Himself heard. Scripture gives witness to the fact that God knows how to talk to people in authority, whether they personally know God or not. "The king's heart is in the hand of the Lord, as the rivers of water: he turneth it whithersoever he will" (Proverbs 21:1).

For women, the problem is an unwillingness to wait for God to take our men out of Satan's hands. Patience is our struggle. Trust, obedience, and an intimacy with our Father are the real issues. Seeking God first above amicable relationships in our homes, work, or school is the bottom line.

When we obey God, God is in a position to deal with those who have been wrong. God does not delight in seeing men crushing women, His chosen vessels. God can deal with fallen men in ways in which we could never dream. As we are submitted and give reverence to the position of authority (even if we cannot give it to the person), God will honor our obedience.

The woman's influence

The godly woman's method is to influence people. She is able to cooperate with others in proper ways. She fulfills this most important role as she draws close to God. She also demonstrates the pearl of great price, which is a meek and quiet spirit. She gives off a sweet fragrance that indeed influences whoever is sent across her path.

A woman has tremendous influence on her children. As she brings forth new life into this world, a woman is able to provide a healthy environment in which this new life may grow. Through this godly environment, children will have the tools to mature and live their lives in dependence upon God. By not having to suffer the consequences of performance-based parenting, they can be tools in the hand of God for their generation.

The power of influence is one of the most important roles of women in both homes and ministry. By example women can influence others to depend upon God. As mentioned in 1 Peter 3:1-5, women can do this without saying a word. Their godly, Spirit-led behavior can win husbands, Christians and non-Christians, over to the Word.

But there needs to be caution

The woman's power to influence can be directed toward good or toward evil. That is very important to understand.

Remember when James talks about "praying with the wrong motives"? You have to be careful you do not fall into this category. When you pray and when you use your influence in someone else's life, please be careful your desires and motives are limited to restricting the power of the enemy and the flesh, not to control another person's will, or impose your particular set of priorities on his/her life.

It happens most often in families. A mother may want her son to go into the ministry, so she prays toward that end without knowing whether that is really God's will for him. A wife may want her husband to volunteer in one of the church's programs, so she nags him about it until he reluctantly gives in or becomes resentful and aloof. These are examples of the power of influence gone awry. Be careful not to fall into these kinds of traps.

Women as teachers

A Christian woman teaches her children. She teaches other children. She teaches younger women. She instructs with her mouth.

Instead of criticizing the young mother who is not feeding the baby right, she offers to help her. She goes by her house and shows her how to fix the formula. She uses her tongue to teach and provide instruction instead of gossiping.

> Likewise, teach the older women to be reverent in the way they live, not to be slanderers or addicted to much wine, but to teach what is good. Then they can train the younger women to love their husbands, to be self-controlled and pure, to be busy at home, to be kind, and to be subject to their husbands, so that no one will malign the word of God. (Titus 3:3-5)

Women in homes and in neighborhoods teach their children to use their anger to fight the real enemy. Women provide protection for their children from evil counsel. By example and instruction, they keep their children from harmful practices. They are selective of the things allowed in the home via TV or the toy box.

Women may also teach the Bible to others. As a woman is growing in the knowledge of the Word, she will be given opportunity to share this with others. She may be given opportunities to teach in Sunday School, churches, conferences and home Bible studies. Boys and Girls clubs, back yard Bible classes and other doors may open to her.

Older women are to teach the younger women how to be self-controlled, pure, keepers of home, kind, and submissive. Many times, one wonders why God did not let people become parents at an older age. Grandparents just seem so much more patient with children. Older women pass on to the younger women the wisdom of experience gleaned from past failures and successes. Younger women can thus benefit from the experience of grandmothers. There is a wealth of knowledge that older godly women can pass on to younger women. Much of our struggles can be lighter as we listen to experiences, successes, and failures of other women.

Women as prophesiers

We will often get a chance to prophesy to the people we pray for. No, not preach at them. We don't mean throwing the Bible at them. We do need to speak God's words of encouragement, comfort and strengthening. That is prophesying according to 1 Corinthians 14:3.

When the newly saved husband comes home drunk, we don't say, "How could you do this to me? I thought you were saved." We say, "Honey, you're a new creation in Christ Jesus. Old things are passed away. We all make our mistakes. I don't know what happened tonight, but I know God still loves you and I'm going to stick by you."

Instead of telling our children they are no good, we tell them they are an heritage of the Lord, and great will be their peace (Psalm 127:3; Isaiah 54:13). That is prophesying.

An encouraging word grounded in the Word is one of the most important keys women have. This godly gift has almost been completely destroyed in many women.

Vine's Dictionary of Biblical Words defines *prophesy* as "speaking forth the mind and counsel of God. It is the declaration of that which cannot be known by natural means. It is the forth-telling of the word of God, whether with respect to the past, present, or future."

As we study the Word of God about what it says about the men and children in our lives, we use it to encourage them. Some do not know God loves them. Others do not know their sins are forgiven. Many do not know God can do exceedingly more than anything they can ask or think. We have the privilege of declaring these and other "Words" to them in a way that will encourage and give them hope.

Sometimes when they are not home, we speak what God says over their rooms. We can declare God's Word over them when they are asleep.

Women will get chances to prophesy in public as well as they are faithful in using the gift in their homes. 1 Corinthians 11:5 specifically identifies women in the public role of prophesying: "And any woman who (publicly) prays or prophesies (teaches, refutes, admonishes or comforts) when she is bareheaded dishonors her head (her husband); it is the same as (if her head were) shaven" (Amplified).

Women as rescuers

African American churches are full of women. Good men are certainly needed in the battle against the enemy.

What can we do? We can play a significant role in rescuing our husbands, brothers, sons, fathers, uncles, and friends.

Are we willing to "stand in the gap" for the men and others in our lives? Are we ready to practice our warfare techniques to free them, even as we are getting free ourselves? Are we ready and willing to release the men in our life and the society in general from the offenses they have brought to us? Are we ready to break the cycles of inferiority, domination, and rejection?

The power to break the cycles is in God. As we submit to God, God can give us victory.

The woman of God realizes many people, even some of her family members, need to be rescued from prisons of immorality, drugs, violence, and even religion, among other things. She is willing to go into these prisons, using the weapons of her warfare obtained in the fiery furnace to release those God assigns to her life.

Because faith without works is dead, women should also be involved in ministering to the needs of others in practical ways (James 2:17). God has prepared works for women to do (Ephesians 2:10). We should be involved not in works to win personal praise from others, but ones others will see and give credit to God in heaven. Then we will be lights shining in darkness, a natural overflow of abiding in Jesus Christ, the Light of the world (Matthew 5:16).

Women can be involved in soup kitchens, making clothes for the needy, tutoring, hospitality, and foster care (Acts 9:39). Many acts of kindness to others are possible. A smile, meal, hug, ride,or a letter are a few of the many ways to administer love.

Women under authority, but also having authority

God wanted women to defeat the enemy. Because of her proposed power over the enemy, she had to be given the most opportunity to be placed under authority. *Those under the most authority have the greatest potential to rightly exercise spiritual authority.*

A woman can legitimately say, even as the centurion in Matthew 8:9 said to Jesus, "I'm under authority and I have those under my authority." As women learn how to be under authority, they can take their positions of authority in the spirit realm.

Real authority has nothing to do with how many people know us. Real authority has to do with how many evil spirits know us (Acts 19:13-16). The kingdom of God is built completely opposite to the kingdom of the world. Authority in the kingdom of God is not based upon how many people you have under you, it is based upon how many people you have above you to serve.

Matthew 20:25-28 records Jesus saying,

> You know that the rulers of the Gentiles lord it over them, and their high officials exercise authority over them. Not so with you. Instead, whoever wants to become great among you must be your servant, and whoever wants to be first must be your slave just as the Son of Man did not come to be served, but to serve, and to give his life as a ransom for many.

Though under authority in the realm of the home, in spiritual warfare, women will be prepared to fight and bring deliverance to women, children, and men—all those who are touched by their lives.

Women under authority exert authority through prayer, the spoken word, and caring acts to effect change over the prisons into which Satan has placed his victims. They will never take a back seat in God's army.

Women, who know God will deal with those who take advantage of them, will learn how to practice submission without fear. They approach God with faith and confidence.

As women watch demons go when they tell them, they understand authority in the spiritual world is much more important than in natural realms. As they realize the purposes of a woman's place, they are thrilled to take theirs in God's kingdom.

Some of these women will garner admiration from others—even pastors and other recognized ministers. But many others who don't get recognition will not mind. They won't care if they do not receive accolades on earth. They smile, knowing Jesus knows, and will publicly acknowledge them in due time.

God can change our cities if just a few women realize their unique value and potential authority in the spiritual realm.

It is time for us to develop a relationship with our heavenly Father based on truth, not lies. We can be a tool in the hand of a faithful God to smash the gates of hell and release many captives.

Danger for women

Unfortunately, whether in her home or with others, a woman's ministry can be easily tainted. It is possible that the Holy Spirit may not be able to flow through her in a pure way. Without this she may do more harm than good in the kingdom of God.

This danger stems from bitterness allowed to root into the spirit because of past offenses. The symptoms include a reluctance to follow the principle of submission and a "chip on the shoulder" about God, men, and other races.

The consequences: little confidence in prayer, misuse of prayer to manipulate people, coming up short in the work of the ministry, fearing other people's opinions, and a tendency to turn back when persecuted.

The bitter woman will fight people and organizations so much she will eventually become useless in destroying Satan's works in the lives of others. Error may begin to enter her message. Without hearing from God about her worth, she will operate out of a sense of inferiority, or will continue to struggle to prove she is capable.

It is so important that all hurts of the past are placed under the blood of Jesus Christ.

It is in the healing process that a woman comes to the understanding of God's love and unique purposes. Once a woman has undergone the healing process successfully, she will be free to be all that God wants her to be in His army.

Hebrews 12:15 says to be careful not to let bitterness root into your soul, ". . . lest many become defiled." It is crucial that the woman of God learn how to see through and rise above the enemy's plan.

Because African American women have so many daily opportunities to become bitter, let us learn to daily walk in the Spirit so we can keep our place in God's army.

Summary

Women have unique roles in the home and in ministry: giving birth, nurturing, defending, rescuing, teaching, prophesying, and influencing others for good. Women have great potential to turn many people back to a dependency upon God. However, they must guard against bitterness and the damage it can do to the work of the ministry.

The possibilities are unlimited when African American women accept God's call to bring defeat to the enemy. The future will definitely hold some "new things" as we learn to live in God's presence and cooperate with Him in unleashing His power into the earth. The next chapter gives us a peek into the future.

Chapter 17

Vision for the future

Remember ye not the former things, neither consider the things of old. Behold, I will do a new thing; now it shall spring forth; shall ye not know it? I will even make a way in the wilderness, and rivers in the desert. **Isaiah 43:18, 19**

How would you like to read the paper or turn on the news and learn that crack houses and abortion clinics were closing due to a lack of customers? Under times of refreshing from the Lord in the past century, saloons closed for the same reason. In past times of revival, churches were packed, and the news media were forced to acknowledge that change was taking place.

Cure for all Ills, by Mary Relfe, will give you a taste of what God has done and a thirst to see it happen again.

The most exciting change is that which takes place in families. Perhaps the following conversations could be from your relatives:

"Mom, I just called to tell you I'm starting to go back to church."

"Son, I want to apologize for the way I treated your Mom during the years you were growing up. I know it wasn't a good example. I

didn't know it then. I was doing what I was taught. I'm praying that God will help you follow His ways with your new wife."

"You know, I just can't get high. I've been using all night. I bet my Mom has been praying again. We might as well stop and try again tomorrow. I'll just call her in the morning and upset her so she'll spend her day worrying instead of praying."

"One time my crazy cousin took care of my kids, and he prayed over my house while I was gone. I poured my bottle of liquor down the toilet when I got home. I don't even know why I did it . . . you know, I've been thinking recently about going to church."

The last incident actually happened. A friend of mine is saved today because of the prayers of her "crazy" cousin.

Ephesians 3:20 says, "[God] is able to do exceedingly abundantly above all that we ask or think according to the power that works in us." *African American women can be keys to change in our families as God's power is at work in us.*

If God is indeed bringing a "new thing" to this nation, it would be helpful to have some idea of how that will affect us. As more people ask God for change, more and more people will see it affect individuals, families, neighborhoods, cities, and this entire country.

Our cities will become safe places to live. The evils such as drugs, violence, murders, unemployment, gangs, and disease that the enemy have brought into our homes and communities will decrease as the enemy is evicted. When God's people wake up and do what God has given them power to do, visible change *will* take place.

Cooperation is key

Though women can be forerunners to change, women and men must work together, complementing each other. Men and women can operate as one unit. When the man is weak, the woman's strength can be there to compensate. And where she is weak, his strength compensates. Tradition will take a back seat in the "new thing."

The result of cooperations should be less dominating, controlling, and manipulating. When Christian men and women learn the proper way of operating together under the one head, Jesus Christ, togetherness can be the rule. As Jesus Christ is in control, unconditional love can erase many of the old ways. Petty jealousies or vying for control will be unheard of in the future.

As women learn to excel in the spiritual arena, giving their lives over to prayer, they can join with men in co-ruling on the earth. Men have traditionally been used by Satan as instruments of damage to women. Is that God's best? No! As women *and* men come into alignment with the purposes of God brought back into the earth through Jesus Christ, we will see men fulfilling their God ordained purpose.

In the home and church community, this purpose is to provide love, cleansing, healing, and protection (covering) as well as physical resources to females (Ephesians 4:25; 1 Timothy 5:3; James 1:27; Acts 6:1).

Gatherings and fellowship

African American women will have to hear from the Lord exactly what the Lord is trying to tell them without interference from others. They may meet to deal with issues that are uniquely theirs. It may mean an even greater interest in conferences for African American women. African Americans may need to come apart in these conferences to hear messages that facilitate getting rid of excess baggage.

As African American women learn to share each other's burdens, they can be transparent with each other. In the "new thing" a lot of healing and growing will take place in more intimate settings. Home fellowships, Sunday School classes, and other small groups will become increasingly important in ministry to women.

We can expect to see a movement of prayer increasing. But praying and teaching are not the only reason to come together. Many of the gatherings will turn into times of singing and testimonies of victory. More time will probably be spent in worship prayers than in petitions as the "new thing" continues because God's blessings will be flowing in abundance bringing healing, deliverance, and peace.

Eventually, we will see African American women strong enough to administer forgiveness to the members of the body of Christ that have been used to reject and ostracize them. They will begin to extend the same covering prayer beyond their own community to others in the body of Christ. They will pray that those whose attitudes of racism have bound them in fear and hatred be released from the sins and influence of their ancestors.

The family of God can begin to function as one and be the force God intended it to be in this world as African American women come into their places.

We have mentioned what God works primarily through people. It is only the power of God that will bring change. He alone has that ability. Recognizing the need and asking God to do it is our part. Other responsibilities of ours include responding in obedience and trusting God for strength for the requested tasks.

The purpose of this book is to facilitate understanding of the process of cooperating with God. We are not suggesting that women go out and make it happen. It is important to let God control our spiritual growth and His purposes through our lives.

The godly, virtuous woman in the "new thing" will know how to walk softly and carry a big stick. She may not shout but Satan will hear her well. God will be ready to send the answers when she prays. She will be known in heaven and in hell.

We close this book with a reminder . . .

Chapter 18

It's time, our time

To every thing there is a season, and a time to every purpose under the heaven. He hath made every thing beautiful in his time: also he hath set the world in their heart, so that no man can find out the work that God maketh from the beginning to the end. Ecclesiastes 2:1,11

Keys are small objects designed by God, the master keymaker, shaped in the fires of pain. Keys are not very significant, or really useful for a lot of things, but they can open locked doors. Without keys, doors remain locked and everything behind them is unavailable. Behind the door may lie vast riches—spiritual and financial blessings, maybe emotional and physical healings.

It is time African American Christian women begin to move forth into what God has called them to be. They hold the key to the door of change in our families, churches, and cities. It is time for us to rise and take our place to facilitate God's healing in this nation. It's time to humble ourselves, pray, seek God's face, and turn from our wicked ways.

Women, it's time to reevaluate all we have experienced through this new understanding and come to Joseph's conclusion: although

Satan meant our slavery and prison experience for evil, God has the ability to bring good out of it all.

It's time to be keys to change

It's time to really know God as our friend. It's time to get ourselves all intertwined in Jesus, standing with Him. It's time to let go of any weights that would slow us down. It's time to have our full dependency in Jesus.

It's time to be shaken out of the traditions of religion and take our place in the body of Christ. It's time to fall in love with Jesus. It's time to experience God's love for us. It's time to allow God to do some major heart surgery. It's time to be vessels of honor, fit for the Master's use (2 Timothy 2:21).

It's time to surrender all to Jesus. It's time to put everything on the altar. It's time to deny ourselves, take up our cross and follow Jesus. It's time to stop playing church and build our house on the solid rock: Jesus Christ.

It's time to stop being a hammer in the hand of the enemy. It's time to refuse to go along with his plan and quit reacting to the hammers Satan uses in our lives by choosing to walk in the Spirit. It's time to know the identity of the real enemy. It's time to get out of the enemy's side and come all the way over to Jesus' side in radical obedience. It's time to say to Satan "enough and no more!"

We can be first. Yes, we can humble ourselves and be the first to say, "Forgive me, I've been wrong holding that against you all these years. I release you. Jesus died for your wrong. It's been paid for. I refuse to hold it to your charge." Even though others have been wrong in judging us by our color and gender, it's time for us to confess the wrong way we have reacted to the injustices.

It's time to admit we have not covered sins with love, nor have we prayed or cried out to God for mercy. It's time for us to do business with our Father. It's time we believe His evaluation of our worth.

It's time to know God freely forgives us for our mistake, faults, weakness and sins. It's time to be aware He's not as bothered about them as we are. It's time to be honest with God, to admit, confess those things hindering us so He can have the liberty to change us. It's time to stop denying, blaming, projecting, minimizing, rationalizing, and making excuses.

It's time to experience Jesus' love, acceptance and forgiveness in spite of our past failures, weaknesses, and mistakes. It's time to walk out of the prison door Jesus has already opened, away from the walls we've built up around ourselves, to freedom. Jesus is giving us that choice. It's time to take it. It's time to make change in spite of pain.

It's time to swallow our pride; It's time to stop pretending. It's time to drop the masks and expose the enemy's work in our life.

It's time to be real with ourselves, with each other and with God if the world is ever going to see Jesus in us.

It's time to stop holding our breath waiting for others to change. It's time to bring God's kingdom to our world.

It's time to regain our places as keepers of our homes and communities, creating an atmosphere of unconditional love, acceptance and forgiveness. It's time to turn away from bitterness and unforgiveness. Instead of sarcasm, criticism, gossip, or slander from our lips, it's time to use our tongues to demonstrate the law of wisdom and kindness—prophesying God's truth. We can use them to pray intercessory prayers.

It's time to be godly influences to our children. It's time to cease from disciplining them out of frustration and anger, continuing negative cycles. It's time to give them the same unconditional love we all crave for. It's time to be kind and patient with them. It's time to have hope and belief in them no matter how many mistakes they have made.

It's our time to lean on Jesus, listening for His secrets and commands and feeling His heartbeat. It's our time to be told the strategy and plan for victory in battle. It's time to use the information received in our prayer closet. It's time to wage spiritual warfare.

With Jesus and His fullness in us, upon us, around us, and for us, it's time we claim our complete restoration and a sevenfold refund on what the enemy has taken from us. It's time to avail ourselves of the power now at our disposal to forgive, get untangled and go forth to free others from their yokes, entanglements, and prisons.

It's time to exercise authority over the plans and purposes of the enemy by staying close to our Master. It's time to seek recognition from Jesus.

It's time to recognize that God is good. It's time to hear Him say, "Well done my good and faithful servant."

It's time to visit the ones caught up in the prisons of drugs, alcohol, homosexuality, and prostitution. It's time to give them the good news that God loves, accepts, and forgives them—and can free them.

It's our time of destiny
When we say that it is our time of destiny, we mean we are destined to be great in letting the captives go free. All those we have held in captivity to their wrongs against us, we now release. Instead of holding them captive, we'll now pray for, bless, and do good unto them.

To those who are exposed to the enemy because of unconfessed sin, we offer "covers" of prayers, and prophecies of comfort. To those who are hungry for unconditional love, we offer a feast at our tables of tenderness, nurture, kind deeds, and understanding. It's time to give refreshing water of healing to the thirsty.

When we say it's our time, we're saying we'll lay down our lives in prayer until the love of God and the truth of His Word breaks through upon others.

When we say it's our time to teach, we mean that it's time to teach warfare techniques and prayer strategies to others. It's time to share life experiences, encouraging others.

It's time to trade pain for a destiny of glory. It's time to experience real joy. It's time to realize the depth of pain and suffering is in direct proportion to our capacity for God's joy and blessings. It's time for the deep crevices of African American women to be filled with God's joy and presence. It's time to receive a double portion of God's anointing as we become clean and chosen vessels, glorifying Him. God is ready to do His greatest work in and through us.

When we say it's our time, we're saying we'll seek His strength. By the grace of God, African American women can be a vital part of the most powerful display of the purposes of God this nation has ever seen.

African American women, it is our time! Let's use it to be salt and light in the world.

African American women, we hold the keys to change. Let's make it our business to use them to God's glory.

IT'S OUR TIME

To everything there is a season
To every purpose there is a time
The God who made the nations
Has everything in His hands
And He wants the world to know Him
Through His love and righteousness
And He's called us to His kingdom
For such a time as this.

Chorus

Now it's our time to believe
It's our time to love and live
There was a time to receive
Now it's time for us to give
Standing hand in hand together
Let's reach out and touch our own
Can you hear the Spirit calling
It's our time.

There was a time we were the learners
Now it's time for us to teach
There was a time for us to follow
Now it's time for us to lead
There was a time we used to borrow
Now it's time for us to feed
It's our world, it's our nation
It's our time of destiny.

We have an obligation
To reach our generation
and pray His kingdom come within our world
And I know we can succeed
Simply cause we do believe
He has given all we need
To carry on.

• by Myles Munroe
(used by permission)

Appendices

Appendix A

Prayer & Bible study guide

This twelve-part prayer is a Scripturally-based way to systematically go through the prayer recipe. It is not meant to be prayed ritualistically, but, like the Lord's Prayer, provides a guide to those who want to make their personal prayer lives effective.

Pay special attention to the Scriptures listed. A systematic review of them would make an excellent Bible study.

1. Father, I admit I have not consistently lived a life of victory over sin, the flesh, Satan, and the world. In my own strength I have not loved you with all of my heart, soul, mind, and strength; neither my neighbor as myself. I agree with your Word that I am powerless to do so (Mark 12:29-31; Matthew 26:41; Romans 7:18;1 John 1:9).

2. I also agree with your Word, Father, you have provided power and resources that I might live an overcoming life. I humbly confess it is no fault of yours. I have not fully availed myself of all you have given (Romans 8:2-4; 2 Peter 1:3; 1 John 4:4; 1 John 5:4; Galatians 5:16; Romans 6:10-14).

3. Furthermore, Father, I've decided continuing in my own strength would be a waste of time. I give you the control of running my life. I turn over to the Holy Spirit through obedience to the Word the tasks of accomplishing your will and revealing Jesus in my life (John 16:7-15; Galatians 2:20; Colossians 1:27; Philippians 1:6, 2:13).

4. Lord, I submit myself into your hands as my judge and give you permission to search my heart. Please bring to light any breaks or bruises there. Expose any wicked ways, hidden works of darkness, and all habits of the flesh, the world system or the enemy (1 Peter 4:17; 1 Corinthians 11:28; Matthew 7:1-5; Psalms 139:23).

5. Father, I also agree to accept the findings of the Holy Spirit and the Word as I am shown faults, weaknesses, sins or other blocks to your life being seen in me. I will admit the truth to myself and also agree to be transparent with others, admitting these findings to them (John 8:28-32; 1 John 1:9; James 5:16).

6. Lord, with your help, I agree to cast aside every weight and sin hindering my walk with you. I agree to take off the old and put on the new by allowing you to transform my mind and emotions. As you show me idols, fleshly patterns, or bondages, I will submit them to your power and your fire (Romans 12:2; Hebrews 12:1; Colossians 3:9,10; Galatians 5:16; Luke 9:23; 1 Corinthians 10:14,20,21).

7. God, I ask for insight into all available provisions for my victory (the blood, cross, Holy Spirit, Word, fellowship and prayer), and I ask you to make them real in my life (Philippians 1:5;2:13).

8. Father, I ask you bring to my memory those whom I have offended. I am willing to restore strained relationships or make appropriate amends. I receive your forgiveness as I now release those who have offended me (Matthew 6:23; Mark 11: 25; 1 John 2:1,2).

9. Lord, I ask you to give me opportunity and guidance to go to those who have wronged me or who I have wronged to seek reconciliation and restoration as soon as appropriate (Matthew 18:15; 5:23-25).

10. I ask you, Father to continue to shine your light on me. I agree to walk in daily fellowship with you and others who are in your family. I agree to submit myself to accountable relationships and admit when I fall short of unconditional love (1 John 1:5-9;4:2-21;1 Corinthians 13:4-7; John 14:34,35).

11. I now present my body, as a living sacrifice to your purposes. In unconditional surrender, I place all aspirations, talents, possessions, people, ministry, beliefs, etc into your hand. I give you permission to either keep them or give them back after purifying my dependency upon them. I turn my life over to your care. Carry out your perfect will in my life, your way and with your power. I want to seek you first (Romans 12:1; Matthew 6:33; Psalms 27:4-8; Jeremiah 29:11).

12. Now, Father, with your strength, I desire to be a bond servant of yours, spreading truth, hope and reconciliation. I will pray for others. I will give words of comfort and encouragement to build up those you bring across my path, especially the difficult ones. I will share what you have done in my life with others. I will but will keep pressing on, refusing to believe I have arrived. giving you the credit for what you do (Mark 16:15; 10:42-45; Matthew 28:19; 2 Corinthians 2:4; 3:4,5; 1 Corinthians 1:26-31; 1 Peter 2:15,16; 2 Timothy 2:20,21; John 12:26;17:1-26).

Appendix B

Recommended books & other resources

I hope CHOSEN VESSELS is only a beginning of the very best God has to offer for many of His chosen vessels. As you journey into the presence of God, you may find a need for additional resources.The following list will provide atibiotic s of truth to individuals who desire to explore in more detail some of the topics brought up in this book.

Some are books from which I have benefited. Others are books that I have discovered in the process of writing this book that confirmed for me the conclusions presented.

The materials listed reflect the diversity in God's family. They are by both women and men, blacks and whites, evangelicals and pentecostals. No one gender, race, or group has all of the answers, but together we can grow into God's purposes. Some of the authors listed have other helpful books.

African American Potential
Carson, Ben with Murphey, Cecil. *Gifted Hands*, Grand Rapids, Michigan: Zondervan Publishing House, 1991.

Edwards, Jefferey. *Chosen—Not Cursed: Destiny of Spiritual Ethiopian.* Tulsa, Oklahoma:Vincom, 1989.

June, Lee; editor. *The Black Family: Past, Present, & Future.* Grand Rapids, Michigan: Zondervan Publishing House, 1991.

McCray, Walter. *The Black Presence in the Bible and the Table of Nations.* Chicago, Illinois: Black Light Fellowship, 1990.

Perkins, John. *Let Justice Roll Down.* Ventura, California: Regal Books, 1976.

Mckissic, William Dwight, Sr. *Beyond Roots :Search of Blacks in the Bible.* Wenonah, New Jersey: Renaissance Productions, 1990

Munroe, Myles. *Understanding Your Potential.* Shippensburg, Pennsylvania: Destiny Image Publishers, 1991.

Hope for Change

Dawson, John. *Taking Our Cities for God.* Lake Mary, Florida:Cretion house, 1989.

Evans, Anthony. *America's Only Hope:Impacting Society in the 90's.* Chicago:Moody Press, 1990.

Relfe, Mary Stewart. *Cure Of All Ills.* Montgomery, Alabama: League of Prayer, 1988.

Swindoll, Chuck. *The Grace Awakening.* Dallas, Texas: Word Publishing, 1990.

Overcoming Satan, flesh, lies, curses, & adversity

Anderson, Neil. *The Bondage Breaker*. Eugene Oregon: Harvest House Publishers, 1990.

Anderson, Neil. *Released From Bondage.* San Bernardino, CA: Here's Life Publisher, Inc., 1991.

Backus, William. *The Hidden Rift with God.* Minneapolis, Minnesota: Bethany House Publishers, 1990.

Benner, David. *Healing Emotional Wounds.* Grand Rapids, Michigan: Baker Book House, 1990.

Frangipane, Francis. *The Three Battle Grounds.* Cedar Rapids, Iowa: Advancing Church Publications, 1989.

Meyers, Joyce. *Tell Them I Love Them: A Message Bringing Revelation of God's Love for You.* Fenton, Missouri: Life in the Word, Inc.,1988.

Peretti, Frank. *This Present Darkness.* Westchester, Illinois: Crossway Books, 1986.

Prince, Derek. *Blessings or Curses: You Can Choose.* Old Tappan, New Jersey: Chosen Books, 1990.

Rinck, Margaret. *Christian Men Who Hate Woman: Healing Hurting Relationships.* Grand Rapids, Michigan: Zondervan, 1990.

Sherrer, Quin and Garlock, Ruthanne. *A Woman's Guide to Spiritual Warfare.* Ann Arbor, Michigan: Servant Publications, 1991.

Prayer

Christenson, Evelyn. *What Happens When Women Pray.* Wheaton, Illinois: Victor Books,1975.

Grubb, Norman. *Rees Howell, Intercessor.* Fort Washington, Pennsylvania: Christian Literature Crusade, 1967 (first published in 1952).

Jacobs, Cindy. *Possessing the Gates of the Enemy.* Tarrytown, New York: Chosen Books,1991.

Murray, Andrew. *With Christ in the School of Prayer.* Grand Rapids, Michigan: Zondervan, 1983 (first published in 1885).

Victorious Christian living

Edwards,Gene. *Living by The Highest Life.* Auburn, Maine: The Seed Sowers Christian Books Publishers House, 1989.

Dawson, Joy. *Intimate Friendship with God.* Old Tappan, New Jersey: Chosen Books, 1986.

Solomon, Charles. *The Rejection Syndrome.* Wheaton, Illinois: Tyndale House Publishers, Inc., 1989.

Stanley, Charles. *How to Handle Adversity.* Nashville, Tennessee: Oliver-Nelson Books, 1989.

Wilson, P. B. *Liberated Through Submission:The Essence of Power.* Pasadena, California: New Dawn Publishing Company, 1990.

Gillham, Anabel. *A Woman's Strength*. Brentwood, Tennessee: Wolgemuth & Hyatt, Publishers, Inc. , 1991.

Nee, Watchman. *The Normal Christian Life.* Wheaton, Illinois: Tyndale House Publishers, 1987.

Nee, Watchman. *The Release of the Spirit.* Indianapolis, Indiana: Sure Foundation, 1965.

Wallis, Arthur. *God's Chosen Fast.* Fort Washington, Pennslyvania: Christian Literature Crusade, 1968

Tape Albums
Beauty for Ashes
Beauty of Submission
Bitterness, Resentments and Unforgiveness
Exposing Strife
Grace, Grace and More Grace
Is Your Mouth Saved?
Let God be God
Lord, Teach Me to Pray
Shaping the Lives of Your Children

Life in the Word, Inc.
Joyce Meyer Ministries
P.O. Box 655
Fenton, Missouri 63026 (314)349-0303

The above tape albums and many other practical teachings are available from this ministry. Write or call for prices and catalog.

Appendix C

About the author

The author, Rebecca Florence Osaigbovo, was born in Tennessee to Thomas and Shermine Florence, who have served as missionaries there since 1950. She is married to Uwaifo Francis Osaigbovo, born in Nigeria.

Rebecca is the mother of three children—a son, Esosa, born in 1980; a daughter, Esohe, born in 1982; and a son, Nosa, born in 1986.

She works part time as a nurse in the substance abuse field. She is also coordinator for Project C.P. R., an organization she founded to mobilize and prepare the church community to fight against the evil of substance abuse and bring hope to those caught in its prison.

Rebecca asked Christ into her life at the age of five and reaffirmed that commitment at the age of twelve. She was challenged to give unconditional surrender to God at the age of sixteen after reading the book, *Rees Howell, Intercessor*. After about six months, she accepted the challenge.

About a month later, shortly after her seventeenth birthday, Rebecca was in the hospital, paralyzed, in a coma, and at death's door. God spared her life through the intercessory prayers of many.

Confident that the prayers of others have been a major factor in God using the next seventeen years to make the unconditional surrender effective and to train her for a ministry as an intercessor—one who speaks to God about people and one who speaks to people about and for God, Rebecca believes in the power of prayer. She is certain praying for others will bring change in our communities.

After graduating from North Park College, Chicago, Illinois in the mid seventies, she began to read extensively to find answers to why Christianity was not really working in her own life and the lives of people of God at large. Her search eventually led to a renewed relationship with God. Her research and experiences form the basis of this book.

After sensing her primary ministry to people would be through writing, she has written four booklets, *It's Time, Ya'll*, 1988; *It's Time to be Transparent*, 1989, *The Role of the Church in Substance Abuse*, 1990 and *A tool in the hand of a faithful God*, 1991.

Additional copies of
*Chosen Vessels: women of color,
keys to change* are available
through your local bookstores.

Ask for it. Give them the ISBN #
1-880560-57-7 (pbk)
1-880560-60-7 (hbk)

Most stores can order it through
their distributors. For a list of
current distributors, stores may
conctact the address below:

Dabar Publishing Company
P.O. Box 35377
Detroit MI 48235

(313) 531-7534 Phone   (313) 531-7535 Fax

To order by credit card, call:
800/628-0903

A HERITAGE OF BLESSING

"A Heritage of Blessing" covers parts of section one and three of *Chosen Vessels*. It is about God's and the real enemy's purposes for women. It gives practical helps to walking in the blessings of God and being a blessing.

"A Heritage of Blessing" Bible Study Guide is available.
"A Heritage of Blessing" seminar is avialable to groups.
"A Heritage of Blessing" audio tapes are available.

Call or write for more information:

Dabar Publishing Company
P.O. Box 35377
Detroit MI 48235
(313) 531-7534

BECOMING A HOUSE OF PRAYER

"Becoming a House of Prayer" covers section two, the
healing process of *Chosen Vessels*. It explores the prayers
that will help us to become a house of prayer instead
of a den of thieves.

"Becoming a House of Prayer" Bible Study Guide is available.
"Becoming a House of Prayer" seminar is available to groups.
"Becoming a House of Prayer" audio and video tapes are available.

Dabar Publishing Company
P.O. Box 35377
Detroit MI 48235
(313) 531-7534

SPREADING THE WORD ABOUT

Chosen vessels: women of color, keys to change

4 ways you can help:

1. If it blesses you, tell others about it.
2. Ask your local library to carry it.
3. Keep an extra copy to loan to others.
4. Give a copy to your church library.

THANK YOU!